■SCHOLAST

M000159707

The Great BIG Book of ☆ Thematic Poetry ☆

by Betsy Franco & Friends

New York • Toronto • London • Auckland • Sydney
Mexico City • New Delhi • Hong Kong • Buenos Aires

Teaching *Resources*

The poems in this collection were originally published as
Thematic Poetry: All About Me! Copyright © 2000 by Betsy Franco
Thematic Poetry: Creepy Crawlies. Copyright © 2000 by Betsy Franco
Thematic Poetry: On the Farm. Copyright © 2000 by Betsy Franco
Thematic Poetry: Neighborhoods & Communities. Copyright © 2000 by Betsy Franco
Thematic Poetry: Transportation. Copyright © 2001 by Betsy Franco
Thematic Poetry: Whatever the Weather. Copyright © 2001 by Betsy Franco

Cover design by Jason Robinson

Interior design by Holly H. Grundon and Ellen Matlach Hassell
for Boultinghouse & Boultinghouse, Inc.

Illustrations by Maxie Chambliss and James Graham Hale

Copyright © 2004 by Betsy Franco

ISBN: 0-439-56729-7

Printed in the U.S.A.

1 2 3 4 5 6 7 8 9 10   40   12 11 10 09 08 07 06 05 04

Contents

Introduction

This multi-themed collection of poems will come in very handy as you look for new ways to enliven the topics you teach. The poetry in *The Big Book of Thematic Poetry* has been thoughtfully written and compiled with preschool to second grade children clearly in mind. Variety, usability, and fun topped the list of considerations in selecting or creating each and every poem.

There are so many ways the poems can be used, so why not get the most you can from each one? Whether you present a poem a week or a poem a day, you can dip into this collection with confidence. You may choose to use the poems in coordination with your phonics program. You can also read aloud the poems, transfer them to a pocket chart, and then let children act them out. In addition, the collection provides jumping off points for writing and connects with science, math, and social studies.

Highlighting Phonemic and Phonic Elements

Poetry and phonics go hand in hand. For instance, look at the rhyming words in the poem "Is That a Star?" (page 146)—*bright, light, right, night*. Transfer this eight-line poem to a pocket chart and then highlight the rhyming words. This can lead nicely into other activities that focus on the long-*i* sound.

In the same way, "Roly-Poly Bug" (page 61) works well for the short-*u* sound, with its rhyming words *bug, hug,* and *snug;* and "A Wave" (page 177) is tailor-made for focusing on vowel digraphs with the long-*e* sound (*me, feet, sea, glee*).

Some poems naturally lend themselves to consonant study. "The Baker" (page 98) has quite a few words that begin with the letter *b*. Introduce the poem "If I Had a Kingdom" (page 37) to your class and have fun with the letter *k*.

Being Authors and Illustrators

Predictable language in poetry can make children feel confident about their own reading and writing. Help children anticipate the rhyming words or repeated phrases in the poems. Then encourage them to go one more step by making up new verses, or poems on similar themes or in similar formats. For example, after reading "Who Am I? (page 101), or "What Is It?" (page 150), invite children to create riddles of their own about city workers or different kinds of transportation.

When a poem looks like what it's saying, as "A Spider Web (page 49), and "Zigzags" (page 62) do, it's called a visual or concrete poem. Another example is "My Extra-Special Box" (page 31), which looks like the box it describes. Let children create their own visual poems. They might create poetry about riding bikes through puddles or leaves, about thunder and lightning, the moon and stars, or fish and other creatures that live in the ocean.

A poem such as "If I Could Build a Town" (page 109) can be duplicated on a page with appropriate blanks for children to complete as shown on the following page. Let children complete this activity individually or as a class. Rhyming is not necessary.

If I could build a town, well then,
I know just what I'd make:

a _____,

a _____,

and a store with _____.

Some poems ask questions. "Your Very Own Design" (page 151) asks children many detailed questions about what kind of vehicle they would design, and "Raindrops" (page 55) asks how they would feel if raindrops were as big as they were—a great invitation to have children engage in writing or dictating.

Why not take a poem and make it into a little foldable book, with one line per page? Children can illustrate each page, making the poem more personal and, therefore, more meaningful. A collaborative class book can be similarly effective. "My Pet Wish List" (page 23) can be a springboard for writing about pets that children wish for, and "The Mixed-Up Farm" (page 86) might spawn a silly book about farm animals making the wrong sounds and then the right sounds.

Building Reading Fluency

Poems provide ideal opportunities for children to practice important aspects of fluency, including phrasing, intonation, automaticity, punctuation, vocabulary, and of course, comprehension. Some poems can be adapted to a call-and-response format in which half the children say some of the lines or verses and the other half complete the lines or verses. You can use "City Traffic" (page 135) this way, and act it out as well. Poems such as "Baby Farm Animals" (page 71), "Waiting for the Bus" (page 134), and "Before the Rain" (page 170) work well in a Reader's Theater or Choral Reading format, with different lines assigned to different children. The animal sounds in "Barnyard Chat" (page 74), the dialogue in "My Friend" (page 99) and the sound-effect words in "Sounds Before School" (page 114) and "Weather" (page 155) let children practice using appropriate expression as they read. Also consider putting poems on tape in a Listening Center for children to follow along as they read copies of the poems.

With many poems in this collection, it can be fun to emphasize the rhyme and rhythm as you read, making them easy for children to follow along. Encourage children to clap, snap, or jump to the rhythm so they can feel the poems in their bodies.

Acting Out Poetry

Dramatic play is another great way for children to explore these poems. They can pretend to be quiet as a butterfly, a snowflake, and a sleeping baby chick in "Quiet" (page 35) or act as if they're in a canoe that turns over in "Don't Rock the Boat" (page 145). Or invite children to perform the suggested fingerplay that accompanies "Here Is the Barn" (page 70). "If You're Happy and You Know It" (page 30) is another natural vehicle for dramatic play.

Creating Science, Math, and Social Studies Links

These poems coordinate wonderfully with all the topics you teach. The sections on bugs, the farm, and weather, for instance, are filled with poems that offer natural tie-ins with science lessons. What a rich body of knowledge can be learned from poems about metamorphosis, baby animals, and types of weather!

Math opportunities abound as well. You can use the poem "Trading at the Bank" (page 111) to explore money and place value. "Car Games" (page 137) lets you introduce counting work in a fun context. "Bee Geometry" (Page 43) and "Rain in the Puddles" (page 168) can lead into a geometry lesson about shapes.

You'll also find social studies connections throughout the collection. Poems about communities and transportation are obvious choices, and "Graphing Families" (page 18) highlights the various sizes and shapes families can take.

This collection includes several multicultural selections to help children appreciate diverse cultures. For example, "Fireflies" (page 58) and "Pretty Little Rooster" (page 76) are traditional Chinese nursery rhymes translated and adapted from the Chinese. And "Languages My Neighbors Speak" (page 97) includes ways to say "hello" in different languages.

Making the School-Home Connection

Poetry always works well as a link to the home. Children can share the poems, their illustrations of the poems, or new verses the class wrote. Poetry is short and easy to read, and it has emotional power for both children and their families.

The treasures in *The Big Book of Thematic Poetry* are yours for the taking. Take advantage of the phonemic and phonic elements, the reading and writing opportunities, and other curricular links—but most of all, enjoy the poetry!

Fireflies

Flickering fireflies,
I see you.
Take these pennies
to buy new shoes.
Your silver's pretty,
Your gold is fine,
But show me how
your bottoms shine.

*Chinese nursery rhyme
translated and adapted by
Betsy Franco and So-Ching Brazer*

All About Me

I'm Special, You're Special

You could search on the land
and search in the sea,
and you'd never find someone
exactly like me.

You could search from Hawaii
to Timbuktu,
and you'd never find someone
exactly like you.

You could travel from China
to Tennessee,
and no one would act
exactly like me.

You could check from Egypt
to Kalamazoo,
and no one would think
exactly like you.

For I am me and
you are you,
I am special and
you are, too.

Betsy Franco

The Great Big Book of Thematic Poetry Scholastic Teaching Resources

Tickles

Tickle your ribs, your chin, your toes.
Tickle your arms with a feather, too.
Tell me—can you tickle you?
Does tickling take one?
   Or does tickling take two?
Everyone knows you can't tickle you—
that in order to wriggle and wiggle,
you need a friend to give you a tickle
that makes you laugh and
   gets you to giggle!

Betsy Franco

A Laugh, A Giggle

a laugh
a giggle,
a "ha, ha, ha,"
a snicker,
a snort,
and a big guffaw
all start with a smile
that lights up your face
and soon you're laughing
all over the place!

Betsy Franco

Which Me to Be

This morning I was late to school
and I can tell you why:
I changed my clothes
so many times—
I just could not decide.

I changed from plain to stripes and then
from blue to red to green.
I wouldn't, couldn't
make up my mind
about which me to be.

Betsy Franco

The Great Big Book of Thematic Poetry   Scholastic Teaching Resources

A Friendly Circle

I taught Kim to build a castle
Kim taught Bo to finger wrestle,
Bo taught Trish to draw a pig.
Trish taught me to do a jig.

You and your friends
could do it, too.
Just teach them what
you love to do.

Betsy Franco

The More We Get Together

The more we get together,
together, together,
The more we get together,
the happier we'll be.
For your friends are my friends,
and my friends are your friends.
The more we get together,
the happier we'll be.

Author Unknown

The Great Big Book of Thematic Poetry   Scholastic Teaching Resources

With a Friend

I can talk with a friend
and walk with a friend
and share my umbrella
in the rain.

I can play with a friend
and stay with a friend
and learn with a friend
and explain.

I can eat with a friend
and compete with a friend
and even sometimes
disagree.

I can ride with a friend
and take pride with a friend
a friend can mean
so much to me!

Vivien Gouled

Making Friends

What's your name?
Would you like to play?
Come and join us.
What do you say?

Betsy Franco

Graphing Families

In class we graphed our families
I counted five in mine—
my parents and my brother
and me and Grandpa Stein.

Some kids lived with their mamas,
Some kids lived with their dads.
Some kids lived with their grandmas
or their favorite granddads.

If we should make a graph again,
then mine'll change to seven,
for yesterday my mom had twins,
my brothers, Dan and Devon!

Betsy Franco

The Great Big Book of Thematic Poetry Scholastic Teaching Resources

Stretching Out My Birthday

On Wednesday,
I brought some cupcakes
to share with kids at school.
On Friday, all my relatives
brought presents that were cool.

I had my party Saturday
with all my favorite friends.
I'd like to stretch it out
so that my birthday never ends.

Betsy Franco

My First Birthday Gift

They didn't give me
a doll or book,
a stuffed giraffe
or game.
On the day
that I was born
my present was
my name!

Sandra Liatsos

In the Middle (according to Terry)

My little brother tells on me,
My older sister teases.
My sister gets the privileges,
My bro does what he pleases.
If I could choose the place I'd be,
I wouldn't choose the middle.
I'd either be the biggest one
or else I would be little.

In the Middle (according to Chris)

My older bro sticks up for me,
My little sister's tough.
He taught me how to bat and pitch,
She shares her toys and stuff.
If I could choose the place to be,
I'd always choose the middle.
It's hard to be the biggest
and I've already been little.

Betsy Franco

Talent Show

We all showed off our talents
at the school talent show,
Each person's good at different things—
as if you didn't know.

Teresa read a funny poem,
and Tommy played the drums,
Rosita's good at magic tricks
and Mei-Mei really hums.

And as for me, I talk a lot—
now that's a real fact.
So I was the announcer who
announced each person's act!

Betsy Franco

My Moves

I can skip
and I can hop
and I can jump a rope.
I can tiptoe,
I can climb
and roll
      right down
         a slope

But when I'm late
I never skip,
I never jump or hop,
I never tiptoe, roll or climb.
I run as fast as my legs will go
to try to be on time!

Betsy Franco

Colors

Colors are pretty. Colors are fun.
Tell me. Which color's your favorite one?

Blue is the sky and blue is the sea.
Yellow's the stripes on a bumblebee.

Red is an apple; white is a blizzard.
Green is the back of a baby lizard.

Black and brown are the garden dirt.
Purple's the throat of a hummingbird.

Orange are the pumpkins out in the sun.
Tell me. Which color's your favorite one?

Betsy Franco

The Great Big Book of Thematic Poetry Scholastic Teaching Resources

My Pet Wish List

I had a list of favorite pets
I hoped my mom would let me get—
a parrot and a kitty cat,
a kangaroo, a baby rat.

My mom said no to all of those
and to a billy goat and crow,
but mom will surely change her mind
when I bring home a buffalo!

Betsy Franco

Playing at Recess

There's running and skipping
and hopping and jumping.

There's shooting and throwing
and kicking a ball.

There's climbing and hanging
and flipping and swinging.

Which one is the one that
you do best of all?

Betsy Franco

What's Cool at School?

Reading
Writing
Math
P.E.
Social studies
Spelling bee
Which one
do you
think is
cool?
What's
your
favorite
thing
in school?

Betsy Franco

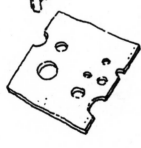

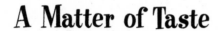

A Matter of Taste

What does your tongue like the most?
Chewy meat or crunchy toast?

A lumpy bumpy pickle or tickly pop?
A soft marshmallow or a hard lime drop?

Hot pancakes or a sherbet freeze?
Celery noise or quiet cheese?

Or do you like pizza
More than any of these?

Eve Merriam

What I'm "Sposed" to Do

When I'm grown up and need to work,
I don't know what I'll do.
I thought about the jobs I've seen,
and listed quite a few:

> I could tend goats,
> mend coats,
> play notes,
> or sail boats.

> I could make pots,
> give shots,
> write plots,
> or care for tots.

> I could fix phones,
> mend bones,
> give loans,
> or polish stones.

My list is nice—I read it twice,
I still don't have a clue.
About the job I'd like the best,
And what I'm sposed to do.
Do you?

Betsy Franco

The Great Big Book of Thematic Poetry   Scholastic Teaching Resources

The Race

I like to run,
I like to race.
Today I did my best.
And I was so much faster
Than I ever would've guessed.

When they said "START"
I moved so fast
I thought that I might burst.
But I huffed and puffed and
tried so hard—
I crossed the finish line FIRST!

Mary Sullivan

The Great Big Book of Thematic Poetry   Scholastic Teaching Resources

Which Animal?

If you could be an animal,
yes, any one at all,
Then you could have a neck so long
it made you very tall.

Or you could crawl like a crocodile
or jump like a kangaroo.
Perhaps you'd like to quack or chirp
or cock-a-doodle-doo?

Or would you like to grow two wings
and soar into the sky?
There're lots of insects you could be
like ants or butterflies.

You'd have a choice of sounds to make
and what you'd like to "wear"—
like feathers, scales and horns and shells
and plain or spotted hair.

Why, you could be a giant whale
or a teeny-tiny flea.
If you could be an animal,
which animal would you be?

Betsy Franco

The Great Big Book of Thematic Poetry Scholastic Teaching Resources

The First Time

I remember the day I blew
my first bubble.
Before that great day it was
lots of trouble.

I remember the day I first
tied my shoe,
It took me a while because
it was new.

I remember the day I first
learned to cook,
but the best of my "firsts"
was reading a book!

Betsy Franco

Feelings

There's happy, embarrassed,
and silly and sad,
There's excited, delighted,
and frightened and glad.

I've had lots of feelings
already today.
And mom says it's only been
half of a day!

Betsy Franco

If You're Happy and You Know It

If you're happy and you know it,
clap your hands.
If you're happy and you know it,
clap your hands.
If you're happy and you know it,
then your life will surely show it.
If you're happy and you know it,
clap your hands.

Author Unknown

The Great Big Book of Thematic Poetry Scholastic Teaching Resources

My Extra-Special Box

A tiny shell, a little
fox, a piece of wax
go in my box.
They're all mixed
up with beads and
rocks inside my
extra-special box.

Betsy Franco

Song of Boxes

Oh, boxes and boxes and boxes
Are fun.
Boxes for rain and boxes
For sun.

Boxes for houses and boxes
For schools,
Boxes for working on
With my tools.

Cages for lions and big tiger cats,
Tables and chairs and special-day hats,
Bridges, tents, and space-monster men,
And boxes for putting boxes in.

Oh, boxes and boxes and boxes
Are fine.
If you don't have boxes,
Come play with mine.

Lillie D. Chaffin

Baby Teeth

I've lost teeth,
and so have you.
The spaces in front,
make it hard to chew.

You've lost four
and I've lost two.
That's six in all,
and we're not even
through!

Betsy Franco

The Great Big Book of Thematic Poetry   Scholastic Teaching Resources

Things That Are Easy

It's easy to lift up my friend in a pool,
It's easy to daydream and doodle at school.

It's easy to slide on a floor in my socks,
It's easy to play in a big empty box.

It's easy to bounce a big red rubber ball,
It's easy to land in the leaves in the fall.

It's easy to giggle, it's easy to laugh,
It's easy to wrinkle when I'm in the bath!

Betsy Franco

Exactly Right

They say that I'm too young
To cross the street to play,
That I'm too old to cry
When I don't get my way,
That I am much too big
To swing on the garden gate,

But very much too small
To stay up after eight.
I'm young, I'm old, I'm big, I'm small—
Do you think, in age and height,
I will ever grow to be
Just exactly right?

Laura Arlon

The Great Big Book of Thematic Poetry Scholastic Teaching Resources

Quiet

I can be as quiet as a spider or an ant,
Quiet as a butterfly;
    Don't tell me that I can't.

I can be as quiet as a little fleecy cloud,
Quiet as a snowflake;
    Now that isn't very loud.

I can be as quiet as a baby chick asleep,
Quieter than that!
    How quiet can you keep?

Walter L. Mauchan

Pocket Treasure

A tiny bit of eggshell
From an empty robin's nest.

It's like a piece of summer sky,
The blue that I like best.

Four fine rocks, one perfect shell,
A rusty little locket—

Those are just a few of the things
In my blue-jeans pocket!

Mary Sullivan

If I Had a Kingdom

If I had a kingdom
then I would be king.
Yes, I would be king
of everything!

We'd each have a kitten,
We'd fly lots of kites,
We'd kick around balls,
and stay up most nights!

If I had a kingdom
then I would be king.
Yes, I would be king
of everything!

Betsy Franco

Smiles Go 'Round

I like to smile.
I like to grin.
I like to be happy-hearted.
'Cause smiles and grins and happiness
Seem to come back to where they started

Mary Sullivan

How People Feel About Me

My aunt says I'm perfect,
My dad says I'm great.
To grandma and grandpa,
I'm really first-rate.

They all clearly like me,
I'm sure you'll agree.
But what's most important
is that I like me.

Betsy Franco

Creepy Crawlies

Bugs All Around

A swarm of
monarch butterflies
is beautiful to see.

Mosquitoes make
a buzzing sound
and so do flies and bees.

The cricket
plays a symphony;
the ladybug is shy.

Most children leave when
gnats or fleas or
spiders are nearby.

The inchworm
and the caterpillar
use their legs to crawl.

The roly-poly
sow bug
curls tightly in a ball.

The walking stick is
hard to see,
but not the firefly.

The dragonfly has
sparkly wings
as it flits swiftly by.

There are so many
bugs around
that I'm surprised to see

there's any space
—on land, in air—
that's left for you and me.

Betsy Franco

Hey, Bug!

Hey, bug, stay!
Don't run away.
I know a game that we can play.

I'll hold my fingers very still
and you can climb a finger-hill.

No, no.
Don't go.

Here's a wall—a tower, too,
a tiny bug town, just for you.
I've a cookie. You have some.
Take this oatmeal cookie crumb.

Hey, bug, stay!
Hey, bug!
Hey!

Lilian Moore

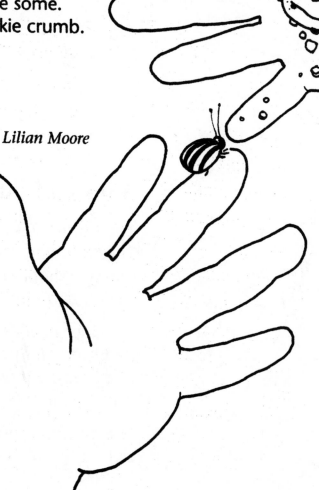

Hurt No Living Thing

Hurt no living thing;
Ladybird, nor butterfly,
Nor moth with dusty wing,
Nor cricket chirping cheerily,
Nor grasshopper so light of leap,
Nor dancing gnat, nor beetle fat,
Nor harmless worms that creep.

Christina Rossetti

Names of Bugs

The butterfly is known to fly,
The glowworm likes to glow,
The grasshopper can hop about
as you and I both know.

But tiger beetles never roar,
and horseflies never neigh.
The firefly, although it's bright,
is not on fire—no way!

The names of bugs may bring delight,
but names of bugs aren't always right.

Betsy Franco

The Great Big Book of Thematic Poetry Scholastic Teaching Resources

Bee Geometry

I'll tell you a secret
between you and me—
The bees must know geometry.

Peek in a beehive
and you will see
the six-sided shapes made by a bee.

The hexagons
you'll find inside
fit side by side by side by side.

I'll tell you a secret,
I think you'll agree—
The bees must know geometry.

Betsy Franco

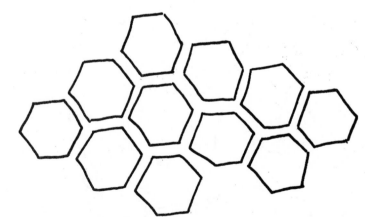

Message from a Caterpillar

Don't shake this
bough.
Don't try to
wake me
now.

In this cocoon
I've work to
do.
Inside this silk
I'm changing
things.

I'm worm-like now
but in this
dark
I'm growing
wings.

Lilian Moore

The Great Big Book of Thematic Poetry   Scholastic Teaching Resources

Butterfly Wings

How would it be
on a day in June
to open your eyes
in a dark cocoon,

And soften one end
and crawl outside
and find you had wings
to open wide,

And find you could fly
to a bush or tree
or float on the air
like a boat at sea . . .
How would it BE?

Aileen Fisher

What About Us Fleas?

Everyone talks
about butterflies,
for the changes
they go through
are such a surprise.

Some changes happen
to fleas like me,
but fleas aren't
beautiful to see,
so no one knows
about the flea.

Betsy Franco

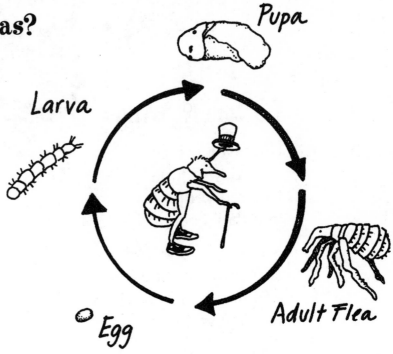

Pupa

Larva

Adult Flea

Egg

O Dearie Me

O dearie me,
Me mother's got a flea,
She put it in the teapot
To make a cup of tea.
The flea jumped out,
Me mother did shout,
In came me brother
With his shirt hanging out.

Author Unknown

The Great Big Book of Thematic Poetry Scholastic Teaching Resources

A Centipede

A centipede was happy quite,
    Until a frog in fun
Said, "Pray, which leg comes after which?"
This raised her mind to such a pitch,
She lay distracted in a ditch,
    Considering how to run.

Author Unknown

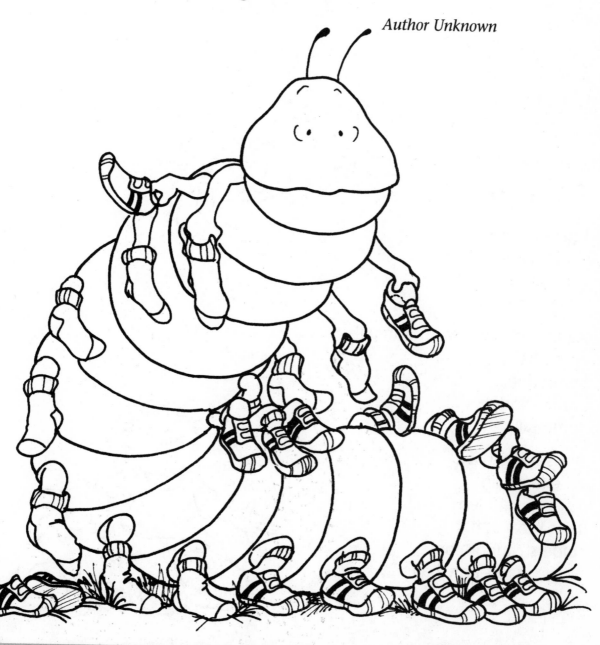

Eensy Weensy Spider

Eensy weensy spider went up the water spout,
Down came the rain and washed the spider out.
Out came the sun and dried up all the rain,
And eensy weensy spider went up the spout again.

Author Unknown

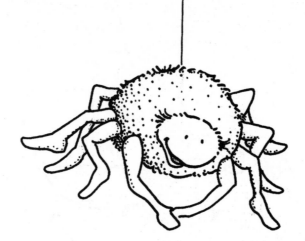

Bug Legs

I have 2 legs.
A cat has 4.
A beetle and a fly
have more.

All insects come with 6 in all—
some hairy,
some thin,
some short,
some tall.

But spiders have
an extra pair.
They have 8 legs in all.
That means that
spiders cannot come
to the insect-only ball.

Betsy Franco

A Spider Web

A spider web is a net of thread for any fly who happens by and doesn't spy the trap nearby. But if the fly is very sly then he'll fly high to pass right by. Then he'll look back and say, "Nice try!"

Betsy Franco

Webs in the Grass

When spider webs are hung with dew
They magically come into view.

Little pixie tents in morning grass,
Like shining nets of silver glass.

But when the sun is hot and bright,
Those webs are hidden from our sight

Like stars that seem to fade away—
Invisible in the light of day!

Mary Sullivan

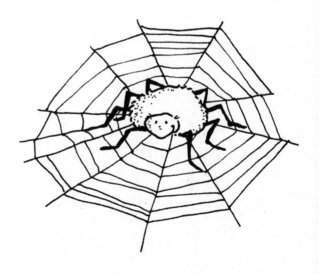

A Cricket, a Flea, and a Bumblebee

A cricket, a flea
and a bumblebee
decided to have an afternoon tea.
Bee brought the honey
as fresh as could be,
Cricket brought the music,
and Flea brought me!

Betsy Franco

The Walking Stick

I saw a stick
that was part of a tree.
That stick began
to walk past me
on six thin legs
and its skin was brown.
It crossed the branch
and started down
the trunk but it never
left the tree,
because it wanted
to hide from me.

Sandra Liatsos

The Great Big Book of Thematic Poetry Scholastic Teaching Resources

Don't Blink

The dragonfly's wings
glimmer and gleam
in the sunny summer sun.

If you blink your eye
as it's zipping by
you may miss a most colorful sight.

For it's almost as fast
as a hummingbird.
It's known for the speed of its flight.

Betsy Franco

Green Grasshopper

A grasshopper hides
   in the green spring grass.
      She knows she blends right in.

You see her when she takes a **h**op
   and shows you where
      she's been.

She disappears
   into the grass
      until she **h**op**s** again.

Don't try to catch her
   just give up,
      'cuz she will always win!

Betsy Franco

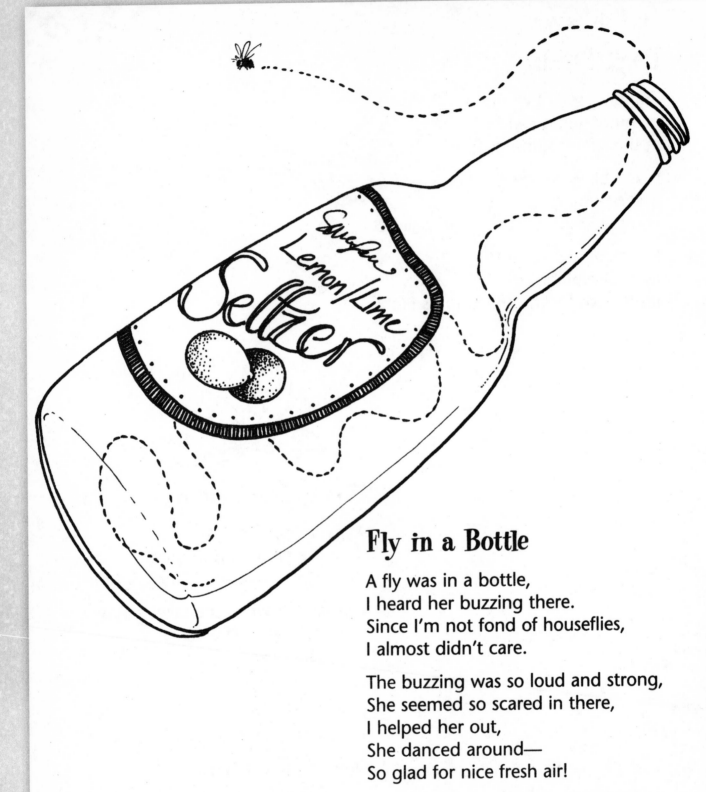

Fly in a Bottle

A fly was in a bottle,
I heard her buzzing there.
Since I'm not fond of houseflies,
I almost didn't care.

The buzzing was so loud and strong,
She seemed so scared in there,
I helped her out,
She danced around—
So glad for nice fresh air!

Betsy Franco

The Great Big Book of Thematic Poetry   Scholastic Teaching Resources

Ants

ants march single-file
when they travel anywhere.

ants find little bits of food
to carry here and there.

ants are very organized
and serious all day.

i wonder if they take time out
to laugh and joke and play?

Betsy Franco

Question for a Ladybug

Come and visit, Ladybug,
dressed in red and polka dots.
I've a question just for you
about the special name you've got—

If you are a father bug,
uncle bug, or brother bug,
do your friends say "ladybug,"
or do they call you "misterbug"?

Betsy Franco

The Great Big Book of Thematic Poetry   Scholastic Teaching Resources

Raindrops

How brave a ladybug must be!
Each drop of rain is big as she.

Can you imagine what *you'd* do
if raindrops fell as big as you?

Aileen Fisher

Bugs on Me

I get wiggly,
I get squiggly,
when an insect
crawls on me,
unless it is a special bug—
a polka-dotted ladybug.
Then I'm as
happy as can be.

Betsy Franco

Pretty Please, Mosquito

Mosquito, mosquito,
you're such a tease.
Please don't bite us
pretty please.
Itchy, scratchy,
scritch, scratch, scritch.
Our arms and legs
all really itch.
You just can't seem to let us rest.
In summertime, you're such a pest!

Betsy Franco

Mosquito

Mosquito whining by my ear,
I can't sleep when you are near!

You buzz and hover by my head,
You circle 'round and 'round my bed!

I pull the covers over my face
And hope you'll
   Soon buzz off
      Some place!

Mary Sullivan

The Great Big Book of Thematic Poetry Scholastic Teaching Resources

The Beekeeper

Our cousin keeps bees.
He wears a long coat
and a hat with a net all around.

Our cousin keeps bees.
He wears his thick gloves
and long pants
that go down to the ground.

Our cousin knows how
to take out the honey
from boxes with hives
full of bees.

Our cousin says, "Have some.
It tastes just like candy."
We eat just as much as we please.

Sandra Liatsos

Letter to Bee

Bee! I'm expecting you!
Was saying Yesterday
To Somebody you know
That you were due—

The Frogs got Home last Week—
Are settled, and at work—
Birds, mostly back—
The clover warm and thick—

You'll get my Letter by
The seventeenth; Reply
Or better, be with me—
Yours, Fly.

Emily Dickinson

The Great Big Book of Thematic Poetry   Scholastic Teaching Resources

Stars With Wings

Sometimes it seems
like all the stars
have fallen
from the skies,
but when I see
the stars have wings
I know they're fireflies.

Betsy Franco

Fireflies

Flickering fireflies,
I see you.
Take these pennies
to buy new shoes.
Your silver's pretty,
Your gold is fine,
But show me how
your bottoms shine.

*Chinese nursery rhyme
translated and adapted by
Betsy Franco and So-Ching Brazer*

The Great Big Book of Thematic Poetry Scholastic Teaching Resources

Cricket Song

The cricket sings
When shadows creep.
His evening song
Says, "Sleep . . . sleep."

I heard this song
From my warm bed.
"Sleep . . . sleep"
Is what he said.

Then very soon
I could not keep
My eyes awake,
So went to sleep.

When morning came
And skies were bright
The cricket's song
Was locked up tight.

But this I know:
When shadows creep,
He'll sing again,
"Sleep . . . sleep."

Elsie M. Strachan

Autumn Concert

In the evening
in the thickets

There are orchestras
of crickets,

And you never
need buy *tickets*

To hear concerts
by the crickets.

Aileen Fisher

Roly-Poly Bug

Hey, roly-poly
potato bug,
why do you act so shy?
When I pick you up,
you give yourself a hug,
and roll in a ball
so cozy and snug!

Betsy Franco

Butterfly Tree

Butterflies
all over the tree
open up and
shine on me,

Butterflies
who warm their wings
and think of sun
the summer brings,

Butterflies
who soon will fly
far to find
their summer sky.

Sandra Liatsos

Zigzags

A butterfly
zigs
    and zags
a lot
    to keep
itself
    from being
caught.

Betsy Franco

What Do You Say to a Bug?

Some say *Ugly!*
Some just *Ugh!*
when they see
most any bug.
But I say, "Yeah!
Let grass-hop, ant-dance, beetle-bop, roly-poly play."

Some say *Ugly!*
Some just *Ugh!*
What do <u>you</u> say
to a bug?

Cynthia Pederson

Calling All Bugs to the Compost Pile

Beetles, fruit flies,
sow bugs, slugs,
spiders, ants,
and other bugs!
Come and live here,
The food is free.
You need no ticket,
There is no fee.
There is no ceiling,
There are no walls.
It's "All-You-Can-Eat,"
You can eat it all!
Beetles, fruit flies,
sow bugs, slugs,
Welcome, welcome,
all you bugs!

Betsy Franco

Under a Rock

Lift up a rock
and you will see
a busy bug
community.

Betsy Franco

The Tiny World

Tiny beetle, busy and black!
Spider creeping across a crack!
Ladybug dressed in a spotted shell!
Grasshopper green, you hide so well!
Wiggly worm in a robin's beak!
Dragonfly buzzing over the creek!
All so tiny, all so small—
To you I must seem VERY tall!

Mary Sullivan

The Great Big Book of Thematic Poetry Scholastic Teaching Resources

The Big Bug Show

They skate on the lake,
  fly down my halls,
climb in the trees,
  crawl on my walls.
They hide in the grass,
  perch on my nose,
buzz on my sleeve
  and hum on a rose.

Sandra Liatsos

Farm

A Farm Visit

My class went to a farm one day,
We touched the soft, brown cow.
We saw where all the milk came from—
I understand it now.

We stroked a chicken's feathers
and we touched a muddy pig.
Her hairs were like a bristly brush,
Her eyes weren't very big.

We watched the goats butt heads
and put their hooves up on the wall.
A little baby lamb was
with her mama in a stall.

We ate some carrots from the ground,
a fresh and healthy snack.
That farm was really neat—
I hope my class and I go back.

Betsy Franco

Early Morning on the Farm

Waking at four
Milking the cows
Gathering eggs
warm from the hen.

Eating fresh eggs
Drinking sweet milk
Then cleaning and feeding
the pigs in their pen.

Betsy Franco

Chores

Digging carrots by the roots,
Counting piglets by their snoots,
Picking up the fallen fruits,
Best be sure to wear your boots.

Marcy Barack

Here Is the Barn

Here is the barn.
Open it wide.
Let's go inside
where the animals hide.

Here are the horses,
Here are the cows.
They're eating their dinner
and drinking right now.

They'll stay here till night
turns into the day.
When we open the doors,
they'll all mosey away.

Out in the pasture
they'll eat grass and hay.
The cows will moo softly.
The horses will neigh.

Betsy Franco

FINGERPLAY *(similar to "Here is the church, here is the steeple . . .")*

1. Make a barn: interlace fingers of two hands inside palms, with thumbs as barn doors.
2. Open up barn by turning over hands to reveal finger horses and cows on each side.
3. Wiggle fingers to show cows and horses moving as they eat their food.
4. Unlink hands to open the barn doors.
5. Have finger cows and horses mosey away.
6. As animals eat in the pasture, raise fingertip heads to moo and neigh.

The Great Big Book of Thematic Poetry   Scholastic Teaching Resources

Baby Farm Animals

A baby horse is called a colt,
A calf's a baby cow.
A piglet is a baby pig,
A mama pig's a sow.

The goslings honk and run around,
The lambs turn into sheep.
The baby goats all kid around,
The kittens play and sleep.

I'm not sure what the farmer calls
a rooster when it's born,
or when it learns to doodle-doo
so early in the morn.

Betsy Franco

Who's on the Farm?

She guards her babies very well.
She nips at people walking by.
She hisses and she honk, honk, honks.
She waddles, swims, and even flies.

Who is she?   (goose)

He has a very wobbly chin.
His wings flap up and down.
Thanksgiving Day, he'd fly away
but he's stuck on the ground.

Who is he?   (turkey)

She chews her cud.
She softly moos.
Her fresh white milk's
her gift to you.

Who is she?   (cow)

Paddle, paddle, paddle,
Dive, dive, dive,
Quack, quack, quack.
It's good to be alive!

Who is he?   (duck)

(Continued)

The Great Big Book of Thematic Poetry   Scholastic Teaching Resources

Who's on the Farm?   *(Continued)*

She hoots and hoots in the barn at night.
She catches lots of mice.
She turns her head this way and that
and blinks her two large eyes.

Who is she?   (barn owl)

Clippity clop, clippity clop.
He lifts his head to neigh.
He's trotting to the big red barn
to eat some fresh-cut hay.

Who is he?   (horse)

She barks and runs around a lot
to herd the sheep together.
She keeps the farmer company
in every kind of weather.

Who is she?   (sheep dog)

Betsy Franco

Barnyard Chat

"Honk, honk."
"Oink, oink."
"Meow, meow."
"Neigh."

"Cluck, cluck."
"Woof, woof."
"Gobble, gobble."
"Bray!"

"Baa, baa."
"Hoot, hoot!"
"Cackle, cackle."
"Moo."

"Quack, quack."
"Peep, peep."
"Cock-a-doodle-doo!"

Stephanie Calmenson

One, Two

One, two,
    The horse needs a shoe.
Three, four,
    The pigs want more.
Five, six,
    Here come the chicks.
Seven, eight,
    Cows at the gate.
Nine, ten,
    A big, fat hen.

Betsy Franco

Pretty Little Rooster

At one o'clock the rooster sings,
At two o'clock he crows.
At 3 and 4, he tells the time.
At 5 he crows and then I know
I must get up and go.

Chinese nursery rhyme
translated and adapted by
Betsy Franco and So-Ching Brazer

In the Chicken Coop

The hens and the rooster
    are huddled together
cramped in the coop
    in the wintry weather,
cackling and clucking
    and pecking each other.
I'm glad none of them
    is my sister or brother.

Sandra Liatsos

Baby Chick

Peck, peck, peck
on the warm brown egg.
Out comes a neck!
Out comes a leg!

How does a chick
who's not been about,
discover the trick
of how to get out?

Aileen Fisher

Chook-Chook-Chook

Chook, chook, chook-chook-chook.
Good Morning, Mrs. Hen.
How many children have you got?
Madam, I've got ten.

Four of them
Are yellow,
And four of them
Are brown,
And two of them
Are speckled red—
The nicest in the town!

Author Unknown

The Barn Cats

In the cow barn
live the cats
who chase the mice
and catch the rats
and when they're done
they get a treat—
two bowls of cow's milk,
warm and sweet.

Betsy Franco

Cows

This morning when the cows woke up,
we milked them in the barn.

The cow's my favorite one of
all the animals on the farm.

Right now they're in the pasture—
some brown, some white and black.

They swish their tails at all the flies
that land upon their backs.

They chew their cud and graze about.
Their eyes are big and kind.

I'm sitting on their pasture fence
and they don't seem to mind.

Betsy Franco

I'm a Little Piglet

I'm a little piglet,
short and stout.
Here is my tail.
Here is my snout.
If another piglet
takes my slop,
I yank his ear
to make him stop.

Betsy Franco

Pink-Skinned Pigs

The pink-skinned pigs
roll in the mud
because it's not much fun
to get a piggy sunburn
in the blazing summer sun.

Betsy Franco

The Great Big Book of Thematic Poetry Scholastic Teaching Resources

Bingo

There was a farmer had a dog
and Bingo was his name-o.
B-I-N-G-O,
B-I-N-G-O,
B-I-N-G-O,
and Bingo was his name-o.

Author Unknown

Bella and Benny

We have two goats
with horns and beards.
They chew most anything—
like old tin cans
and table scraps
and bark and corn and beans.

Those silly goats
eat all day long.
They never get enough.
And when they play
they butt their heads
and act like they're so tough.

Betsy Franco

Horses

Back and forth
and up and down
horses' tails go switching.

Up and down
and back and forth
horses' skins go twitching.

Horses do
a lot of work
to keep themselves from itching.

Aileen Fisher

Bathing Puddles

It rained last night,
The ground's all wet.
The cows leave puddles where they've been.

For ducks, those puddles
are just right
for quacking, splashing, bathing in.

Betsy Franco

Baa, Baa, Black Sheep

Baa, Baa, Black Sheep,
Have you any wool?
Yes sir, yes sir,
Three bags full.
One for my master,
One for my dame,
And one for the little boy
who lives in the lane.

Author Unknown

To Market

To market, to market,
To buy a fat pig;
Home again, home again,
Jiggety jig.

To market, to market,
To buy a fat hog;
Home again, home again,
Joggety jog.

Author Unknown

The Great Big Book of Thematic Poetry   Scholastic Teaching Resources

Sheep on the Loose

"The sheep got loose,
The sheep got loose!"
loudly honked
the farmer's goose.

The chickens pecked
the sheep's thick wool,
the goats all pushed,
the ducks all pulled.

The rooster called
the sheepdog Jack
and sure enough,
Jack had the knack.
He made those silly sheep go back.

Betsy Franco

woof!

The Mixed-Up Farm

The farm got
all mixed up one day.
The piglets mooed,
The sheep said, "Neigh."

The rooster barked
to ask for food,
The goats all cock-a-doodle-dooed!

The farmer worked
all day and night
to straighten out the farm again.

The pigs said, "Oink."
The horse said, "Neigh."
But "Moo, moo, moo," said mother hen.

Betsy Franco

On an Apple Farm

It's time for apple cider,
And for roasted apples, too,
And taffy apples
Sitting on a stick.
I'd rather have October
Than April, May, or June,
For we've apples
By the bushel we can pick.

Sandra Liatsos

What
kind of apples
are sticky and
crunchy and
easy to hold
in your

h
a
n
d
?

Betsy Franco

Sitting on the Tractor

High in the tractor,
my dad waves to me.
He's plowed all the fields
and he's sowing the seed.

In fall in the thresher,
he'll harvest the grain.
In spring, he'll be plowing
the fields again.

Betsy Franco

The Great Big Book of Thematic Poetry   Scholastic Teaching Resources

Pumpkin Patch

The sunlight hits the hillside where
the farmer's pumpkins grow.
They're bright, bright orange
with vines of green.
They're sitting out in rows.

Some big, some small, some weirdly shaped,
some rough, some smooth and round,
I pick my favorite of the bunch.
They weigh it by the pound.

When we get home, I'll scoop it out
and roast the pumpkin seeds.
I'll carve my jack-o-lantern's face.
How scary it will be!

Betsy Franco

Family Garden on the Farm

Corn and beans,
Corn and beans,
Silly scarecrows in between.
Cukes and lettuce,
Cukes and lettuce,
We can eat them when they let us.
Sweet green peas,
Sweet green peas,
Munch and crunch them, as we please!

Betsy Franco

The Great Big Book of Thematic Poetry   Scholastic Teaching Resources

Grandmother's Garden Song

Carrots, onions,
Parsnips, kale—
If you'll come help me
We'll soon fill the pail.

Peas in the springtime,
Pumpkins in fall,
Beans in the summer—
Food for us all.

Patricia Hubbell

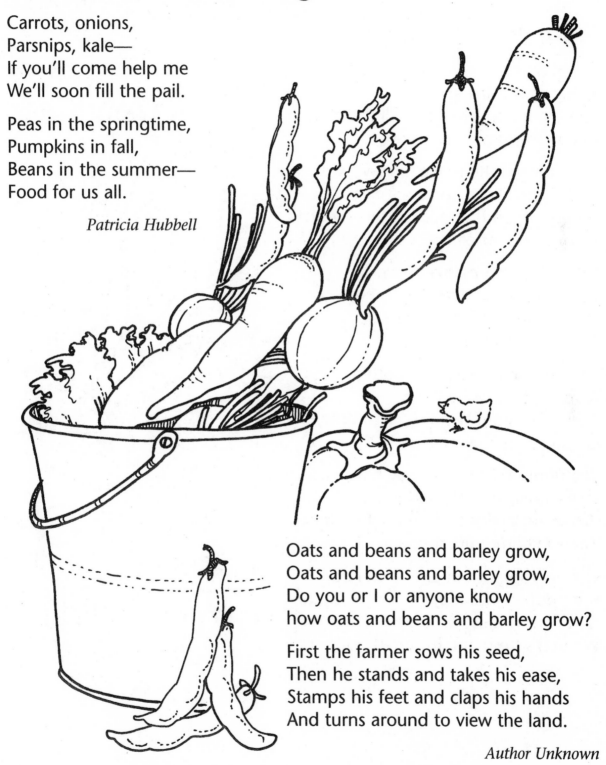

Oats and beans and barley grow,
Oats and beans and barley grow,
Do you or I or anyone know
how oats and beans and barley grow?

First the farmer sows his seed,
Then he stands and takes his ease,
Stamps his feet and claps his hands
And turns around to view the land.

Author Unknown

Down on the Corn Farm

When great-great-grandpa had a farm,
A hundred years ago,
The men and boys grew all the corn
And work went rather slow.

They turned the fertile furrows with
A plow behind a horse,
And dropped the seeds in one by one,
All by hand, of course.

Nowadays, on mama's farm
you'll see some different scenes.
My mama and her workers do
Their jobs on big machines.

The fields are leveled smooth as rugs
Across a hardwood floor,
And rows are plowed ten at a time,
Or sometimes even more.

The farming methods may have changed
As years have come and gone,
But some things still remain the same:
The sun comes up at dawn;

The ears sprout out and fatten up,
Are popped into a pot;
And corn is most delicious
When it's fresh and buttered hot.

Joy N. Hulme

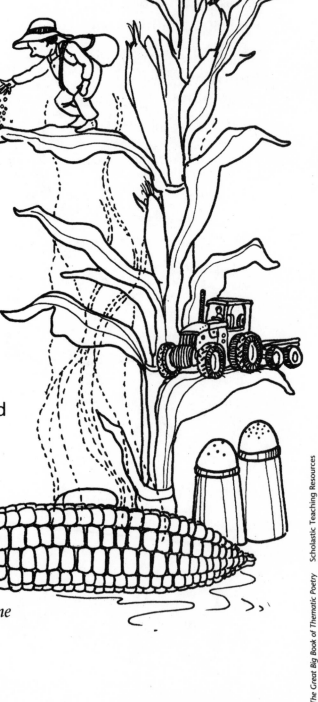

The Great Big Book of Thematic Poetry Scholastic Teaching Resources

Food's Found

On vines
   Grapes and pumpkins
   grow on vines—
   thick as ropes—
   or on thin green lines
   as do squash
   and all of these:
   tomatoes, cucumbers,
   melons, and peas.

On trees
   orchards offer
   all who come
   apple, cherry,
   peach and plum;
   grapefruit, orange,
   lemon, limes
   (these, of course,
   in tropic climes),
   apricot,
   and fig, and date—

fruits we all
appreciate.
nuts the nut trees
will provide—
even coconuts,
round and wide.
hungry?
just look at the trees
loaded down
with delicacies!
Underground
   carrots, potatoes,
   and turnips grow
   deep under the ground—
   though green leaves show—
   and so do parsnips,
   and yams and onions. but
   would you think to look
   there for a peanut?

Elsie S. Lindgren

Breakfast on the Farm

Jersey cow, if you please,
Give us cream to make some cheese,
Jersey cow, don't moo and mutter,
Give us cream to make some butter!

Little chicken, if you please,
Give us eggs for an omelet (cheese!).
Little chicken, if you are able,
Give us eggs for the morning table!

Mary Sullivan

Community

Some Folks in a Town

a takeoff on "Rub-a-Dub-Dub"

Ding-a-dong down,
Some folks in a town,
And who do you think they be?
The dentist, the baker,
the computer-parts maker,
the teacher, the nurse, and me.

Ding-a-dong down,
More folks in the town,
Now let me tell you who—
the policewoman's here,
the firefighter's there,
the mailman's next to you.

Ding-a-dong down,
More folks in the town.
So how many do you see?
Librarians, bus drivers,
doctors, and grocers,
We're all a community!

Betsy Franco

Languages My Neighbors Speak

The man at the shoe repair
    speaks Spanish
      Buenos Dias.

The lady at the bakery
    speaks French
      Bonjour.

The man at the falafel stand
    speaks Hebrew
      Shalom.

The lady at the fish market
    speaks Japanese
      Konichiwa.

Chinese, Swahili, Russian, Greek—
any language that I seek
are languages my neighbors speak!

                  Linda Bendor

The Baker

The baker leaves
before the sun
to bake the bread,
both white and wheat,

and cakes of chocolate,
dark and sweet,
and sticky rolls
and chocolate treats.

His baking makes
the lovely smells
that make his baked goods
sell so well.

Betsy Franco

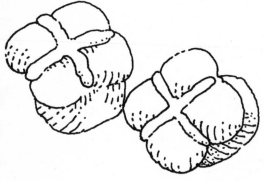

Hot-Cross Buns

Hot-cross buns, hot-cross buns,
One a penny, two a penny,
Hot-cross buns.
Who ate a bun?
You are the *one*.

Author Unknown

The Great Big Book of Thematic Poetry   Scholastic Teaching Resources

Firefighters

The firefighters have to dress
with special hats and boots.
When fighting fires, they need to wear
their fireproof gloves and suits.

A firefighter's truck is red
and makes a siren sound
so all the cars will let it by
when there's a fire around.

If you should need a firefighter
someday when you're at home,
just call the numbers 9-1-1.
The fire truck will come!

Betsy Franco

My Friend

Mailman Jim is my good friend.
He brings to us what people send,
Letters, postcards, presents, too,
And best of all, sometimes, he says,
"Today there's one for you!"
"Thank you very much," I say.
"Have a very happy day."

Tomorrow I'll give Mailman Jim
A special letter just for him.

Sandra Liatsos

Police Officers

The police must be there
    night and day
so we are safe at school
    and play.

On motorcycle, horse,
    or car,
they wear a badge wherever
    they are.

They're here to help us,
    you and me.
They protect our whole
    community.

Betsy Franco

The Great Big Book of Thematic Poetry   Scholastic Teaching Resources

Who Am I?

I look at your teeth
To see they're all right.
Then give you a toothbrush
To help keep them white.
Who am I?

(dentist)

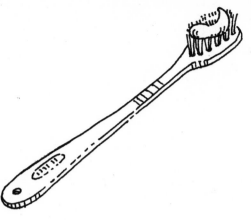

Is your hair getting shaggy?
Come in, take a seat.
I'll cut it and comb it
To make it look neat.
Who am I?

(barber or hairdresser)

Climb aboard my yellow bus.
We'll ride to school and then,
When your school day's over,
I'll drive you home again.
Who am I?

(school bus driver)

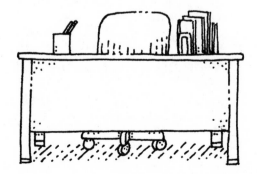

You'll find me in your classroom
When the school bell rings.
I'm always there to help you
so you can learn new things.
Who am I?

(teacher)

Stephanie Calmenson

The Great Big Book of Thematic Poetry   Scholastic Teaching Resources

Visits to the Doctor

The doctor fixed my broken arm,
and once she gave me stitches.
She gives me medicine to take
when poison ivy itches.

But checkups at the doctor
that just make me want to cheer
are when the nurse says, "That's all, Joe,
You won't need shots this year!"

Betsy Franco

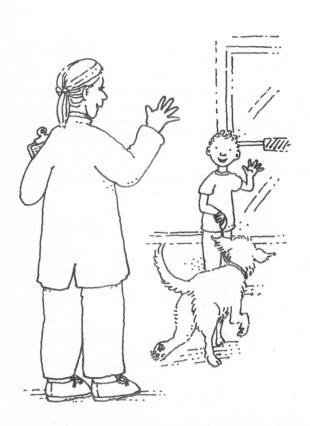

The Vet
to the tune of "Little Bo-Peep"

The vet sees pets,
like cats and dogs.
Her job is just to help them.
And when she's done,
she sends them home,
wagging their tails behind them.

Betsy Franco

The Great Big Book of Thematic Poetry   Scholastic Teaching Resources

Ice Cream Man

If I were old enough to drive
I'd be an ice cream man.
I'd paint delicious
ice cream colors
on my ice cream van.
My bell would clang,
a loud, loud clang
up and down the streets.
When kids came running,
I'd have fun
selling ice cream treats.

Sandra Liatsos

The People at School

An apple for my teacher
who teaches us each day,
A flower for Ms. Rosa
who watches us at play.

A purple plum for Mr. Keys
the friendly maintenance man,
He fixes all the broken stuff
and keeps things spic and span.

A peach for the librarian
who reads us books each week
and lets us take home picture books
to borrow, not to keep.

An orange for the secretary—
she's always very cool,
A drawing for the principal
who runs the whole big school.

Betsy Franco

The Great Big Book of Thematic Poetry Scholastic Teaching Resources

My Neighborhood

People move in,
People move out,
Little children play and shout.
Old people, young people,
in between,
make a lively neighborhood scene.

Betsy Franco

The Sidewalk

The sidewalk's free to anyone,
The sidewalk runs around the town.

It's very straight for one whole block,
and then it curves and curves around.

There's room to play a hopscotch game
or draw on it with colored chalk.

For dogs it is a meeting place
when people take them for a walk.

Some kitties think the sidewalk space
is just the place to lie right down.

When sidewalk squares get slick with ice,
there's lots of people on the ground.

Some say it's bad to step on cracks;
I use that rule I must admit.

The sidewalk is a special place,
I wonder who invented it.

Betsy Franco

bumping up the curb   bumping down the curb

That's what I like to do   on my bike

Betsy Franco

Homes

Homes can be trailers,
Homes can be boats,
Home is the place
where you hang your coat.

Homes are apartments
and mansions and tents.
Homes can be wooden
or stone or cement.

Homes can be large,
Homes can be tall,
Homes can be cozy and
friendly and small.

Wherever you live,
if it's old or it's new,
your Home is your
"Home sweet Home" to you.

Betsy Franco

If I Could Build a Town

If I could build a town, well then,
I know just what I'd make:
an ice cream store, a toy shop,
and a store with bread and cake.

I guess I'd make a park
and build a nifty fire station.
Say, would you like to help me?
It just takes imagination!

Betsy Franco

Supermarket, Supermarket

A jump rope rhyme

Supermarket, supermarket,
shelves piled high
with brand-new products
for you to buy:

Vegetable soapflakes,
filtertip milk,
frozen chicken wings ready to fly,

shreddable edible paper towels,
banana detergent,
deodorant pie.

Eve Merriam

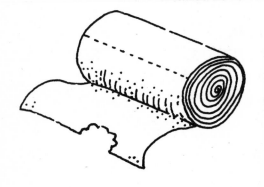

The Great Big Book of Thematic Poetry Scholastic Teaching Resources

Best Deal in Town

I go to the library after school
and find myself a book that's cool.
There is no charge,
The books are free.
Just how much better could it be?

Betsy Franco

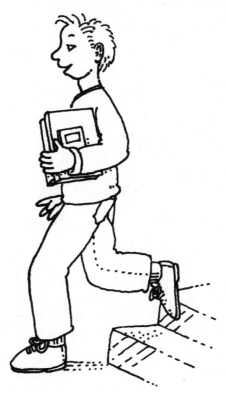

Trading at the Bank

I went to the bank with my pennies—
with all of the pennies I'd earned.
I wrapped them and stood in a very long line,
then waited and waited my turn.

I traded my pennies for dollars.
I walked a few blocks down the street.
I met my best friends at the bakery shop
and bought everybody a treat.

Betsy Franco

Going to the Mall

We start at the toy store
and walk down each aisle—
some stickers, some whistles,
a glass crocodile.

Then off to see jewelry
like black spider rings,
a watch, and a bracelet,
and sparkly things.

We look through the pet store
at turtles and mice,
The puppies and kittens
and hamsters feel nice.

We walk through the mall,
and there's so much to do.
Each time that we go there,
we see something new.

Betsy Franco

The Great Big Book of Thematic Poetry   Scholastic Teaching Resources

On the Way to School

We started to school,
just my sister and I.
We walked and we talked,
watched the birds in the sky.

We walked across Green Street
and added two more—
Teresa and Pedro
and then there were four.

We turned the next corner
with two blocks to go,
Some more kids joined in and
we watched the group grow.

Before we were through,
there were eight kids in all,
just walking to school
on a morning in fall.

Betsy Franco

Sounds Before School

Ka-boom, ka-boom,
a bouncing ball
slamming up against the wall,
Low notes from a clarinet,
Orange ball *swishing*
through the net,
Ty and Bobby calling Hope,
The sound of someone *skipping* rope.
First bell *rrrings.*
Doors open wide.
We *scuffle* our feet
and *shuffle* inside.

Betsy Franco

Main Street

The bookstore,
the sports store,
the grocery,

The post office,
bank, and the
library,

The firehouse,
the clinic,
the town police.

The pet store,
the shoe store,
the bakery.

I gave you
a tour all along
our main street.

Now don't you
agree that
our city is neat?

Betsy Franco

The Great Big Book of Thematic Poetry   Scholastic Teaching Resources

Wake Up

In the country
Everyone knows
It's morning when
The rooster crows.

But the city's
A different matter!
You're sure to hear
Garbage cans clatter,
Taxis toot,
Buses roar,
A paper slap
Against your door.

In country or city,
Morning sounds say,
"Wake up! Here comes
Another day."

Eva Grant

City Fingerplay

Tall shop in the town,
Lifts moving up and down.
Doors swinging round about,
People walking in and out.

Author Unknown

> Have children do this fingerplay
> with the poem:
>   raise hands above head,
>   move hands up and down
>   swing arms from side to side
>   move fists back and forth

Note: Tell children that *lifts* are elevators.

The Great Big Book of Thematic Poetry   Scholastic Teaching Resources

116

Sharing the Road

From the window of our school bus,
    we can see the busy road.
There's a dump truck and a tow truck
    and a pickup with a load.

There's a fire truck! Police car!
    Now I see the ice cream man!
There's a mail truck and a sports car
    and a white delivery van.

There are cars and trucks and bicycles,
    a giant city bus.
We can see them out the window
    as they share the road with us.

Betsy Franco

Construction

The giant mouth
chews
rocks
spews them
and is back for
more.

The giant arm
swings up
with a girder
for
the fourteenth floor.

Down there,
a tiny man
is
telling them
where
to put a skyscraper.

Lilian Moore

The Great Big Book of Thematic Poetry   Scholastic Teaching Resources

Crossing the Street

Traffic lights are meant to be
Safety lights for you and me:
    Green means GO!
      First look each way!
Yellow—WAIT!
    A slight delay!
Red means STOP!
    And stop right then
    until it's green,
    then go again!
So every time we cross the street
Let's watch the lights and tell our feet!

Vivian Gouled

It Fell in the City

It fell in the city,
It fell through the night,
And the black rooftops
All turned white.

Red fire hydrants
All turned white.
Blue police cars
All turned white.

Green garbage cans
All turned white.
Gray sidewalks
All turned white.

Yellow NO PARKING signs
All turned white
When it fell in the city
All through the night.

Eve Merriam

The Great Big Book of Thematic Poetry　Scholastic Teaching Resources

The Key to the Kingdom

This is the key to the kingdom.
In the kingdom there is a city.
In the city there is a town.
In the town there is a street.
In the street there is a yard.
In the yard there is a house.
In the house there is a room.
In the room there is a bed.
On the bed there is a basket.
In the basket there are flowers.
    Flowers in the basket,
    Basket on the bed,
    Bed in the room,
    Room in the house,
    House in the yard,
    Yard in the street,
    Street in the town,
    Town in the city,
    City in the kingdom . . .
And this is the key to the kingdom.

Author Unknown

A City Goes to Sleep

The moon watches over the city at night.
The city goes out, light by light.
The buildings are quiet, not even a peep.
The city is slowly going to sleep.

Some animals sleep in the bushes and parks
while others are roaming around in the dark.
The bark of a dog, the toot from a car,
The clankety sound of the last streetcar.

The fire and police station buildings are lit
but most other workers have called it quits.
The sidewalk is empty, the moon is bright.
The city is falling asleep for the night.

Betsy Franco

Transportation

Transportation

Cars, trucks,
rockets, planes,
canoes, boats,
bikes, and trains.

Motorbikes, buses,
skateboards, feet,
subways, taxis,
trolleys in the street.

So many ways
to travel around:
in water, in air,
or down on the ground.

We'll fly to Mars
or rocket to the moon
in passenger spaceships
very, very soon.

We can drive or pedal
or walk or row.
Transportation takes us
wherever we go!

Betsy Franco

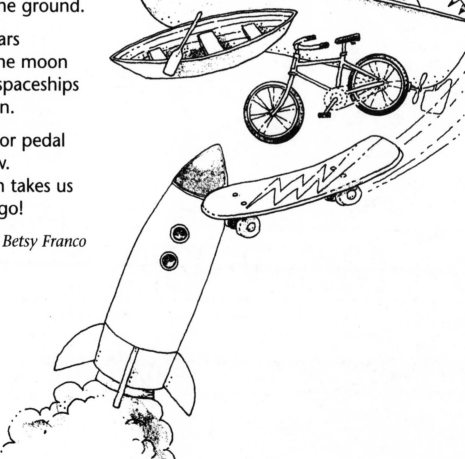

Speed

A rocket's faster
than a jet.
A jet moves faster
than a plane.
A plane is faster
than a boat.
It's also faster
than a train.
A train moves faster
than a horse.
A horse moves faster
than a mule.
But mornings
when I'm really tired,
I'd like to ride a mule to school.

Betsy Franco

An Exciting Trip

I ride the elevator up
In our apartment house
And no one knows I'm playing
For I'm quiet as any mouse.

But I pretend I'm piloting
A rocket, swift as light,
That's full of passengers I'll land
Upon the Moon tonight.

When we ride down,
my rocket ship
Falls like a shooting star,
And lands upon the Earth again
Without the slightest jar.

The other people never know.
As up and down we flip.
That I am taking them upon
A wild, exciting trip!

Frances Gorman Risser

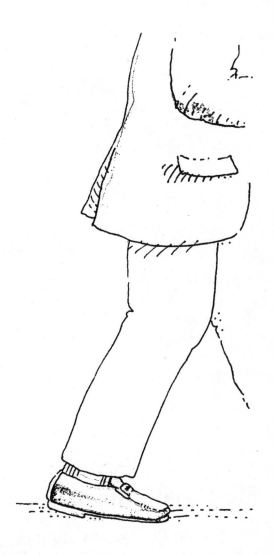

Walking

Father's legs are very long.
He seldom walks for fun.
He mostly walks for getting there,
which makes *me* have to run.

Aileen Fisher

Growing Up on Wheels

I had a toy car
to ride down the hall,
then a shiny, blue trike
that was sturdy but small.

My brand-new bike
with training wheels,
seemed to me
like a pretty big deal

until I learned to
ride on my own,
and now I pedal
to school alone.

When I'm grown up,
I'll drive a car
and visit my friends
wherever they are!

Betsy Franco

My Cousin Ronny Zips Around

My Cousin Ronny zips around—
he has a fancy wheelchair.
He presses buttons with his hands
to travel here and travel there.
His wheelchair takes him near and far,
to all the places he's explored.
Whenever I see him 'round the town,
he says that I can hop on board!

Betsy Franco

Rainy-Day Detective

I never knew
how my mother could tell
that I rode through puddles
on rainy days.

Then I looked in
the mirror
and I said, "Hey!"

"It's the stripe
on my back
that gives it away!"

Betsy Franco

Thematic Poetry: Transportation Scholastic Professional Books

Roller Skating

Swing, glide, sway, and roll,
Watch for the cracks and jump the hole.
Over the walks, under the trees,
Skating along as fast as I please.

Clump, clump! Over the grass,
Stepping aside for the ladies to pass.
Swing, glide, roll, and sway,
Skating is fun on a sunny day.

Frances Arnold Greenwood

All Downhill

I wish my town was all downhill,
with lots of open space.
I'd wear a hat and grab my sled
to get from place to place.
I'd take a running start and jump,
and down the hill I'd race,
while snowy, chilly winter winds
were blowing in my face.
I'd have a special "lifter" at the bottom
just in case
I didn't want to climb back up
all the way to my starting place.

Betsy Franco

At the Bike Rack

When you leave your bikes at the bike rack,
just what do you think they do?

Do they figure out who's old and new?
Do they count how many are green and blue?

Do they talk about how their tires are flat,
that they have a new basket, and things like that?

Do they talk about all their bruises and bumps
and how their riders like to jump?

When you leave your bikes in the bike rack,
don't you sometimes wish you knew

what all those bicycles talk about
and what they say about you?

Betsy Franco

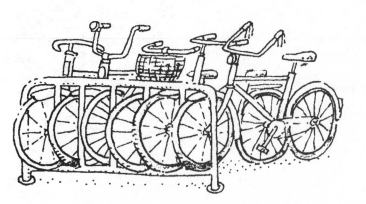

The Wheels on the Bus

The wheels on the bus
go 'round and 'round
'round and 'round
'round and 'round.
The wheels on the bus
go 'round and 'round
all through the town.

Author Unknown

Coming to School

I take a bus.
Barb rides her bike.
Coming by car is what
some children like.
Ralph always runs.
Dawn has to hike.
The ways that we come
are not all alike.

But . . .
Monday through Friday,
in fall, winter, spring,
we're lined up and ready
when morning bell rings!

Betsy Franco

Waiting for the Bus

We're waiting for the bus,
the yellow, bug-eyed bus;

backpacks sitting in a bunch,
lunchtime sandwiches all crunched.

I wish that bus would HURRY UP
before this waiting gets too much!

Gabby's doing last night's work.
Matthew eats today's dessert.

Hector's spitting pumpkin seeds.
Lindy's chasing broken beads.

I wish that yellow, bug-eyed bus
would come and take us

off the street!

Jacqueline Sweeney

City Traffic

Beep, honk, step on the brake.
City traffic makes us wait.

Taxis dodging here and there.
Cars and vans are everywhere.

Buses pick up girls and boys.
Trucks look like they're giant toys.

Blinking stoplights flash and glow.
City traffic's stop and go.

Pull to the right for the siren sound.
Fire trucks are all around.

Traffic stops while a car gets towed.
Lots of people cross the road.

City traffic's really cool,
but I hope that I'm not late for school!

Betsy Franco

The Wheel

How very strangely we should feel
If someone had not made a wheel!
No wagon would have crossed the plain,
No puffing engine, no speeding train.

No cart or carriage would there be,
Or roller skates for you and me,
No bicycle or automobile,
If someone had not made a wheel.

Josephine Van Dolzen Pease

The Great Big Book of Thematic Poetry   Scholastic Teaching Resources

Car Games

Car rides are usually boring.
Car rides aren't usually fun.
But Mimi and I know lots of games
that are great for everyone.

We play the alphabet-license game.
We sing about ants marching two by two.
We look for e x t r a-w i d e, v e r y l o n g trucks,
and we hunt for all the numbers, too.

In cities, we count the phone booths.
We count all the cows in the countryside.
And while we're playing game after game,
the car-riding time just seems to fly!

Betsy Franco

Stopping to Look at Trucks

Everyone stops to look at trucks—
grandpas, babies, moms, and dogs,
kids just on the way to school,
someone taking a morning jog,

'cuz trucks crunch
and lift
and pump
and whirl.
They scoop
and dig
and sweep
and twirl.
They beep, beep, beep when backing up.
They lift up workers in the sky to fix the wires way up high.

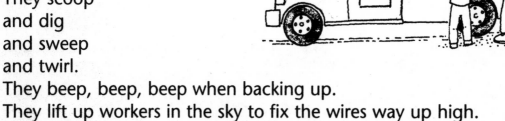

Everyone stops when a truck is near
'cuz there's so much
to look at
and
so much to hear!

Betsy Franco

The Great Big Book of Thematic Poetry   Scholastic Teaching Resources

Noisy Eater

Clash
crash
bang
bash
crunch
munch
squeal.
The recycling truck
just came by our street
to eat its morning meal!

Betsy Franco

Fire Truck

Clang! Clang!
Fire truck coming!
Racing down the street.
Fire in a building.
Feel the heat!

Jump from the truck.
Connect the hose.
Whoosh! Whoosh! Whoosh!
There the water goes.

The people are safe now.
So is their cat.
The fire is out.
How about that?

Stephanie Calmenson

Subway

Here come tiger down the track
ROAR-O
Big white eye and mile-long back
ROAR-O
Through the darkest cave he run
ROAR-O
Never see the sky or sun
ROAR-O

Lillian Morrison

Lazy-Day Train Ride

We step on the train.
The whistle blows.
The engine lurches
and off we go.

Our tickets are punched.
We settle back.
The train is chugging
down the track.

We pass by towns.
The bells ring out,
and people watch us
on our route.

We have no plans—
it's Saturday.
We'll ride to the end
and back today.

Betsy Franco

Engine

Work, little engine,
    Pull us along;
Puff, little engine,
    Puff a gay song!

Work, little engine,
    Pull, pull, pull!
Draw forth cars
    That are full, full, full!

Work, little engine,
    Blizzard or rain;
Puff, little engine,
    Pull the long train!

Nona Keen Duffy

A sailor went to sea sea sea
To see what he could see see see.
But all that he could see see see,
Was the bottom of the deep blue sea sea sea.

Author Unknown

Sailing With Whales

Sailing along in the morning wind
my father and I rode out to sea.
The gulls around us circled and cried,
around and around my father and me.
We were the only ones in sight
except for the whales and the salty foam.
We sailed in the wind for hours and hours
before we had to head back home.

Sandra Liatsos

The Great Big Book of Thematic Poetry Scholastic Teaching Resources

Don't
rock the
boat—I'm
warning you.
Just paddle the
way I asked you
to. Or you'll turn
over our little
canoe and out
we'll fall—me
and you, into
the water
cold and
blue!

Betsy Franco

Row, row, row your boat
gently down the stream.
Merrily, merrily, merrily, merrily,
Life is but a dream.

Author Unknown

Is That a Star?

Is that a star
by the crescent moon?
It's very bright
with a flashing light.
It can't be a star.
It doesn't look right.
It's an airplane
flying by at night!

Betsy Franco

Window Seat

Up we went like a soaring hawk
and everything got very small.
The cars and homes and roads and pools
looked like a map you see in school.
The clouds took over after that—
they floated softly by.
The ground just disappeared from view
'cuz we were up so high.
But, I saw the Rocky Mountains
and the Mississippi, too.
I *always* pick the window seat
to get the bird's-eye view!

Betsy Franco

Helicopter Morning

Whirley-bird, whirley-bird,
loudest bird I ever heard
clattering above my bed,
metal feathers on your head
spin their noisy song of steel.
Whirley-bird, you make me feel
as if I'll never fall asleep,
so out of bed I'll quickly leap
to watch you squawking up the sky.
I see your pilot waving, "Hi."

Sandra Liatsos

I'd Like to Rocket

I'd like to rocket
through the sky
and look down
on my planet's face.

I'd be the first
kid-astronaut
to make her way
through outer space.

Sandra Liatsos

Up in the Space Shuttle
(A True Story)

When my neighbor rode up
in the Space Shuttle,
he said the earth
looked beautiful.

He studied the sun
with his feet strapped down
and floated about
to move around.

He's glad to be home,
but now and then,
he says he'd like
to do it again.

Betsy Franco

What Is It?

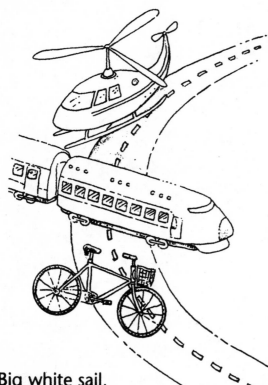

"All Aboard!"
Clackity-clack.
We go speeding
down the track.
What is it? _____ (train)

With seat belts on,
we drive around.
We stop and go
all over town.
What is it? _____ (car)

Up in the sky,
above the clouds,
propeller whirring,
fast and loud.
What is it? _____ (helicopter)

Betsy Franco

Big white sail,
wind in my face.
Over the waves
we bump and race.
What is it? _____ (sailboat)

Pedals twirl
and wheels turn.
We ride to school
and then return.
What is it? _____ (bicycle)

Across the lake
I row and row.
The harder I pull,
the faster I go.
What is it? _____ (rowboat)

The Great Big Book of Thematic Poetry   Scholastic Teaching Resources

Your Very Own Design

If it was completely up to you,
and you could design a plane, boat, or car,
what would you build?
How would it look?
Think of all the colors there are!

How many wheels or wings or sails?
Think about size. How big would it be?
Would it be different?
Would it be wild?
Would it be meant for land, air, or sea?

What would you call it?
How fast would it go?
How would it move?
Would you steer? pedal? row?
If it was completely up to you,
what would you make?
What would you do?

Betsy Franco

Storybook Travel

If I could go inside a book
and travel like they do,
I'd travel in a magic way.
How about you?

Would you ride inside a pumpkin-coach,
like the one in *Cinderella*?
Or would you be like Mary Poppins,
riding her umbrella?

Would you ride like Harry Potter,
on a broom up in the sky?
Or would you rather fly a magic carpet
way up high?

If I could go inside a book
and travel like they do,
I would choose the magic carpet.
How about you?

Betsy Franco

Nighttime, Rest Time

The trains are asleep
in the station.
The boats are docked
in the bay.
The airplane lights
look just like stars.
It's the end of nice, long day.

The bikes are in garages.
The skates are under beds.
Most everything is resting
for a busy day ahead.

Betsy Franco

The Great Big Book of Thematic Poetry   Scholastic Teaching Resources

Weather

Checking Out the Weather

I check out the weather
as soon as I can
'cuz it helps me each day
when I'm making a plan.

Is it puddle-hop, sledding,
or ball-playing weather?
Is it time to wear boots,
or no shoes altogether?

Are the clouds big and puffy
or heavy and dark?
Should I plan to stay in
or go play at the park?

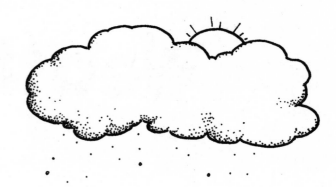

Is the temperature high?
Is the temperature low?
Is it sunny or stormy
or ready to snow?

I check out the weather
as soon as I can
'cuz it helps me each day
when I'm making my plan!

Betsy Franco

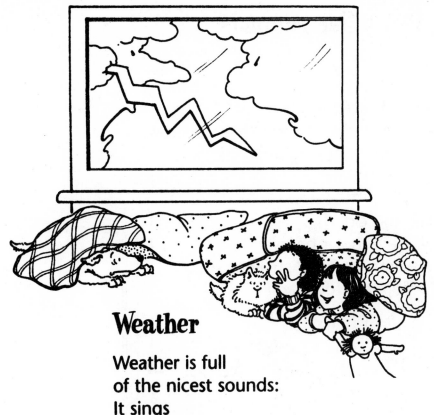

Weather

Weather is full
of the nicest sounds:
It sings
and rustles
and pings
and pounds
and hums
and tinkles
and strums
and twangs
and whishes
and sprinkles
and splishes
and bangs
and mumbles
and grumbles
and rumbles
and flashes
and CRASHES.

Aileen Fisher

The Great Big Book of Thematic Poetry Scholastic Teaching Resources

How Pam Picks Her Pajamas

Pam has pajamas
with daisies and roses
and rainbows and butterflies, too.
She wears them whenever the weather's been warm
and the sky has been sparkling and blue.

Pam has pajamas
with snowflakes and clouds,
and with furry, white polar bears.
Whenever the weather's been chilly or snowy,
she picks *those* pajamas to wear.

Betsy Franco

Predicting the Weather

Our tin can
measures snow and rain.
For wind we have
a weather vane.

We read the clouds
and the temperature.
With *all* these tools,
we're still not sure!

Betsy Franco

The Great Big Book of Thematic Poetry   Scholastic Teaching Resources

The Animals' Favorite Weather

Gators love to lie about
in the heat of the noontime sun.
Penguins dressed in black and white,
think freezing cold is fun.

Polar bears love snow and ice,
but geese fly south where weather's warm.
A knot of toads croak loud and clear,
all wet and happy, in a springtime storm.

Betsy Franco

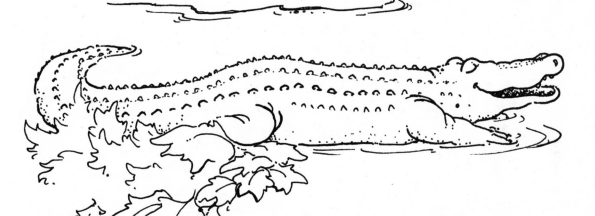

My Cat, the Weather Reporter

He's fat and furry when it's cold outside.
He's thin and sleek in the summertime.
He's jumpy and scared before they report
that a thunderstorm is coming to town.
And when the fall leaves swirl and twirl,
he chases and races all around.

Betsy Franco

Leaf Blankets

Leaves are falling, soft as snowflakes,
Red and yellow, gold and brown;
The breeze laughs gaily in the treetops,
Shaking all the color down.

Leaves are covering the gardens
As my blanket covers me.
When cold winter comes, the flowers
Will be warm as warm can be.

Irene B. Crofoot

The Great Big Book of Thematic Poetry   Scholastic Teaching Resources

Back to School

When summer smells like apples
and shadows feel cool
and falling leaves make dapples
of color on the pool
and wind is in the maples
and sweaters are the rule
and hazy days spell lazy ways,
it's hard to go to school.

But I go!

Aileen Fisher

The Wind in Fall

The wind is like a street sweeper,
that gathers up the leaves.
I wish that it would sweep them all
in a pile for you and me.

We'd build a giant fortress.
We'd jump and howl and roar.
We'd invite the wind to play with us
and we'd never ever get bored.

Betsy Franco

As Soon As It's Fall

Rabbits and foxes
as soon as it's fall
get coats that are warm
with no trouble at all,
coats that are furry
and woolly and new,
heavy and thick
so the cold can't get through.

They don't have to buy them
or dye them or try them,
they don't have to knit them
or weave them or fit them,
they don't have to sew them
or stitch them all through . . .

They just have to GROW them,
and that's what they do.

Aileen Fisher

The Great Big Book of Thematic Poetry   Scholastic Teaching Resources

Snow

Snow blows
In bunches.
Snow sparkles
And crunches.

Snow is clean and cold.
Snow is crisp, and yet
When it warms a little,
Snow is wet.

Any winter day, I know,
Is pleasanter when there is snow.

Lillie D. Chaffin

Walking Home on a Snowy Day

Catching snowflakes on your tongue,
Tapping on a snow-filled oak,
Walking in a trail of prints,
Breathing puffs of dragon smoke.

Making angels on a lawn,
Falling forward in the snow,
Sliding on an icy walk,
Lining snowballs up to throw.

Those are things I like to do
when the snow is thick and new.

Betsy Franco

Zero Degrees

Your cheeks,
your nose,
your fingers,
your toes
all feel it the most
when the temperature goes
to zero degrees
or somewhere
below.

Betsy Franco

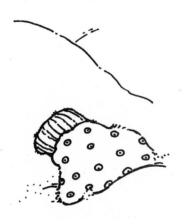

The Thoughts of a Winter Mitten

She's sliding on the driveway,
she's falling off her sled,
she's rolling down the hillside,
she's standing on her head.
She's lost me in a snowdrift
and doesn't even see.
Until the weather changes,
this snow is where I'll be.
Poor me!

Betsy Franco

Snow Friends

I make a snow boy, and a girl.
They like the crispy, crunchy weather.
Their smiles are wide.
They raise their arms.
They're glad I made them close together.

But when the sunshine warms them up,
they melt and shrink,
their arms sag down.
There's really nothing I can do.
Their silly smiles turn into frowns.

"Don't worry now," I tell them both.
"'Cuz even if you melt away,
I'll build you both back up again
as soon as there's
a snowy day!"

Betsy Franco

Skating on a Winter Pond

Freezing fingers lace my skates.
Pulling tight, while cold ice waits.

On frozen pond, push off quick.
Sliding,
    gliding,
        skate blades click.

Twirling,
    whirling,
        curving round,

Spinning,
    speeding,
        slapping sound.

Cutting patterns, figure eights.
Winter pond beneath my skates.

Joan Cottle

Wrapped in a Quilt

There's no better place
than wrapped in a quilt
when the weather is blustery, flustery;
when the window is
covered with icy-cold lace
and you don't have to get up
and be anyplace.

Betsy Franco

Bird Songs

Oh, there's music
In the forests
And there's music
In the glen
As the birds
Are warbling greetings
To the spring
That's come again.

Anonymous

Spring Things

The baby birds are hatching
and learning how to sing.
Somehow the weather gives them clues
and tells them that it's spring!

Then when they have their feathers
and learn to flap their wings,
they jump into the bright, blue sky
and try
      the "flying thing!"

Betsy Franco

Rain in the Puddles

Circles here,
Circles there,
No triangles,
rectangles,
diamonds
or squares.
Just
circles
on
circles
everywhere!

Betsy Franco

The Playful Windshield Wipers

On rainy days, when we're driving around,
the windshield wipers like to play.
They play in a drizzle; they play in a storm.
They love it when the weather's gray.

They move together back and forth.
They like to move at different paces.
They always play a game of tag
and challenge each other to all sorts of races.

They have a special job to do—
they wipe and swish the rain away.
But windshield wipers never touch,
no matter which game they choose to play!

Betsy Franco

Before the Rain

Patch the cat gets kind of jumpy,
round and round goes the weather vane,
Grandma's knee begins to ache
whenever it's about the rain.

Sam the spaniel starts to bark,
the tree branch taps the windowpane,
the wind chime plays a lively tune
right before it starts to rain.

Betsy Franco

Rain Plus Sun

A rainbow
happens
when
two kinds
of weather
decide
to *celebrate*
together.

Betsy Franco

After the Rain

The houses drip,
the trees drip,
and though the rain
is through,
the fences drip,
the dogs drip,
and I am dripping, too.

Sandra Liatsos

The Great Big Book of Thematic Poetry   Scholastic Teaching Resources

Spring

First day of spring;
On the ancient plum tree
Three open blossoms.

Lorraine Ellis Harr

Spring Haiku

Rows of rain droplets
on the empty spider web.
Where is the spider?

Betsy Franco

When the Wind Rushes

When the wind rushes,
    Swirling and sweeping,
Little white clouds
    All wake from their sleeping.
Across the bright sky
    They tumble and fly
To play with the kites
    That are jiggling by.

When the wind rushes,
    Dipping and dancing,
The clothes on the clothesline
    Start leaping and prancing.
They rattle their clothespins
    And away they all fly,
To play with the clouds
    And the kites in the sky!

Patricia Hubbell

Wind

When mischievous wind
sneaks up on crisp autumn leaves—

          they scuttle like crabs

Liza Charlesworth

The Great Big Book of Thematic Poetry   Scholastic Teaching Resources

When I See Clouds

The puffy clouds mean sunny days.
The whispy clouds mean rain's in store.
The sky can be all striped with clouds.
The black clouds say it's going to pour.
But what I see when I see clouds
is a hippo, a sheep, and a moose with horns,
and cotton candy—giant-size—and
sometimes even a unicorn!

Betsy Franco

Clouds

White sheep, white sheep
On a blue hill,
When the wind stops
You all stand still.
When the wind blows
You walk away slow.
White sheep, white sheep,
Where do you go?

Christina G. Rossetti

The Smells of Summer

There are certain things in summer
That smell real nice to me.
The moss and ferns and woodsy things
I like especially.

The grassy lawn just freshly cut,
The fragrant stacks of hay,
The clean outdoors when it has rained,
The salty ocean spray—

Pine needles warming in the sun,
Fresh corn, and berries, too,
Bright flowers in a big bouquet—
I like these smells, don't you?

Vivien Gouled

Busy World

Bees are buzzing, frogs are hopping,
Moles are digging. There's no stopping
Vines from climbing, grass from growing,
Birds from singing, winds from blowing,
Buds from blooming. Crickets humming,
Sunbeams dancing, raindrops drumming.
All the world is whirling, dizzy—
Summertime is very busy!

Frances Gorman Risser

Running Through the Sprinkler

You can let the water chase you,
there are lots of games to play
when you're running through the sprinkler
on a hot and muggy day.

You can sit right on the squirt holes,
you can run every-which-way,
and it's fun to wear your school clothes—
never mind what Mom will say.

You can stand still as the water comes
or jump across the spray.
Just picking up the sprinkler
can chase everyone away.

If your friends come by to see you,
you can ask them all to stay
when you're running through the sprinkler
on a hot and muggy day.

Betsy Franco

The Great Big Book of Thematic Poetry   Scholastic Teaching Resources

Ramona Street on a Hot Summer Day

You can hear the whack
of a tennis ball against the plastic bat.
You can smell Mrs. Lowry's
honeysuckle bush.
You can lick an ice cold popsicle
from Pete's ice-cream truck.
You can feel Mr. Garcia's sprinkler water
tingling on your warm skin.
There's no place I'd rather be
than Ramona Street
on a hot summer day.

Betsy Franco

Summer Cooking

July is steaming the world today
People and places are cooking away. . .
Sizzling, baking, boiling, roasting,
Can't you feel that your toes are toasting?

Sandra Liatsos

At the Seaside

When I was down beside the sea
A wooden spade they gave to me
  To dig the sandy shore.

My holes were empty like a cup
In every hole the sea came up,
  Till it could come no more.

Robert Louis Stevenson

A Wave

I sat on the beach and a beautiful wave
  Came tumbling right up to me.
It threw some pink shells on the sand at my feet,
  Then hurried straight back out to sea.

It ran away swiftly and leaped up in foam;
  It bumped other waves in its glee.
I think it was hurrying to gather more shells,
  To bring as a present to me.

Gussie Osborne

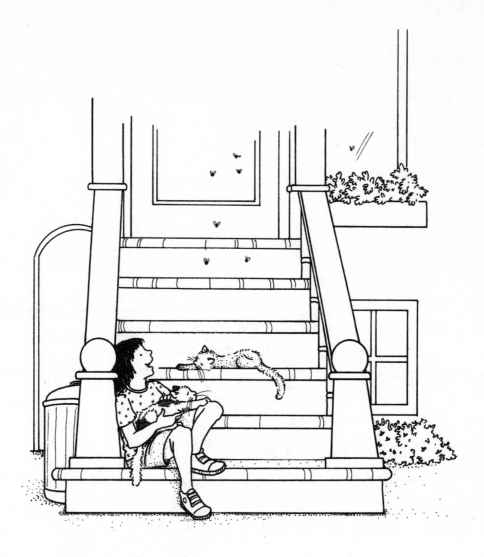

Summer Night

A summer evening's lovely
With its shadows blue and deep
And its busy crickets strumming
Drowsy songs to make us sleep.

With its flitting fireflies glowing,
With its stars so big and bright,
And its gentle breezes sighting
Little secrets through the night.

Jean Brabham McKinney

The Great Big Book of Thematic Poetry Scholastic Teaching Resources

What Kind of Weather?

In winter when it falls on you,
you always look surprised.
But when you try to catch it,
it just melts before your eyes.
What's falling? _____ (snow)

It can steal your hat.
It can blow your hair.
It can make the leaves
dance here and there.
What's blowing? _____ (wind)

It pitter-patters on the roof.
It waters garden flowers.
When we go out without a coat,
it gives us all a shower.
What's coming down? _____ (rain)

Puffy, white pillows
fill the sky.
They hold the rain
way up so high.
What's up there? _____ (clouds)

Rumble, rumble,
boom, boom, boom,
Dazzling light
fills up the room!
What's happening? _____ (thunder and lightning)

Betsy Franco

Different Places, Different Weather

My pen pal lives in Cleveland.
I live in San Francisco.
When I have lots of winter rain,
my friend has slush and sleet and snow.
In spring, we both have daffodils
and wind and sun and whippoorwills.
In summertime, I don't have rain.
In Cleveland it's just not the same.
In fall her trees light up the sky.
Mine aren't so bright—I don't know why.
So. . .
in autumn, I go see her trees,
and wintertimes, she visits me!

Betsy Franco

The Great Big Book of Thematic Poetry   Scholastic Teaching Resources

Wait for Me

Wait for me
and I'll be there
and we'll walk home together,
if it's raining
puddle pails
or if it's sunny weather.

Wait for me
and I'll be there
and we'll walk home together.
You wear red
and I'll wear blue
and we'll be friends forever.

Sarah Wilson

ACKNOWLEDGMENTS

ALL ABOUT ME

LAURA ARLON. "Exactly Right" by Laura Arlon. Copyright © 1990 by Scholastic Inc. Used by permission of the publisher.

LILLIE CHAFFIN. "Song of Boxes" by Lillie D. Chaffin. Copyright © 1990 by Scholastic Inc. Used by permission of the publisher.

VIVIAN GOULED. "With a Friend" by Vivian Gouled. Copyright © 1990 by Scholastic Inc. Used by permission of the publisher.

SANDRA LIATSOS. "My First Birthday Gift" by Sandra Liatsos. Copyright © 1991 by Sandra Liatsos. Used by permission of Marian Reiner for the author.

WALTER L. MAUCHAN. "Quiet" by Walter L. Mauchan. Copyright © 1990 by Scholastic Inc. Used by permission of the publisher.

EVE MERRIAM. "A Matter of Taste" from THERE IS NO RHYME FOR SILVER by Eve Merriam. Copyright © 1962, 1990 by Eve Merriam. Used by permission of Marian Reiner for the author.

MARY SULLIVAN. "The Race," "Pocket Treasure," and "Smiles Go 'Round" by Mary Sullivan. Copyright © 1999 by Mary Sullivan. Used by permission of the author.

CREEPY CRAWLIES

SO-CHING BRAZER. "Fireflies" translated from the Chinese by Betsy Franco and So-Ching Brazer. Copyright © 2000 by Betsy Franco and So-Ching Brazer. Used by permission of the authors.

AILEEN FISHER. "Autumn Concert" and "Raindrops" from OUT IN THE DARK AND DAYLIGHT by Aileen Fisher. Copyright © 1980 by Aileen Fisher. "Butterfly Wings" from IN THE WOODS IN THE MEADOW IN THE SKY by Aileen Fisher. Copyright © 1965, 1993 by Aileen Fisher. All are reprinted by permission of Marian Reiner for the author.

SANDRA LIATSOS. "The Walking Stick," "The Beekeeper," "Butterfly Tree," and "The Big Bug Show" by Sandra Liatsos. Copyright © 2000 by Sandra Liatsos. Used by permission of Marian Reiner for the author.

LILIAN MOORE. "Hey, Bug!" from I FEEL THE SAME WAY by Lilian Moore. Copyright © 1967, 1995 by Lilian Moore. "Message from a Caterpillar" from LITTLE RACCOON AND POEMS FROM THE WOODS by Lilian Moore. Copyright © 1975 by Lilian Moore. Both are reprinted by permission of Marian Reiner for the author.

CYNTHIA PEDERSON. "What Do You Say to a Bug?" by Cynthia Pederson. Copyright © 2000 by Cynthia Pederson. Used by permission of Marian Reiner for the author.

MARY SULLIVAN. "Mosquito," "Webs in the Grass," and "The Tiny World" by Mary Sullivan. Copyright © 1999 by Mary Sullivan. Used by permission of the author.

ELSIE M. STRACHAN. "Cricket Song" by Elsie M. Strachan. Copyright © 1990 by Scholastic Inc. Used by permission of the publisher.

FARM

MARCY BARACK. "Chores" by Marcy Barack. Copyright © 2000 by Marcy Barack. Used by permission of Marian Reiner for the author.

SO-CHING BRAZER. "Pretty Little Rooster" translated and adapted by Betsy Franco and So-Ching Brazer. Copyright © 2000 by Betsy Franco and So-Ching Brazer. Used by permission of the authors.

STEPHANIE CALMENSON. "Barnyard Chat" by Stephanie Calmenson. Copyright © 2000 by Stephanie Calmenson. Used by permission of Marian Reiner for the author.

AILEEN FISHER. "Baby Chick" from RUNNY DAYS, SUNNY DAYS by Aileen Fisher. Copyright © 1958, 1986 by Aileen Fisher. "Horses" from UP THE WINDY HILL by Aileen Fisher. Copyright © 1953, 1981 by Aileen Fisher. Both reprinted by permission of Marian Reiner for the author.

PATRICIA HUBBELL. "Grandmother's Garden Song" by Patricia Hubbell. Copyright © 2000 by Patricia Hubbell. Used by permission of Marian Reiner for the author.

JOY N. HULME. "Down on the Corn Farm" by Joy N. Hulme. Copyright © 2000 by Joy N. Hulme. Used by permission of the author.

SANDRA LIATSOS. "In the Chicken Coop" by Sandra Liatsos. Copyright © 2000 by Sandra Liatsos. By permission of Marian Reiner for the author. "On an Apple Farm" by Sandra Liatsos appeared originally in THE VINE. Copyright 1980 by Graded Press. Used by permission.

ELSIE S. LINDGREN. "Food's Found" by Elsie S. Lindgren. Copyright © 1990 by Scholastic Inc. Used by permission of the publisher.

MARY SULLIVAN. "Breakfast on the Farm" by Mary Sullivan. Copyright © 1999 by Mary Sullivan. Used by permission of the author.

COMMUNITY

LINDA BENDOR. "Languages My Neighbors Speak" by Linda Bendor. Copyright © 2000 Linda Bendor. Reprinted by permission of the author.

STEPHANIE CALMENSON. "Who Am I?" by Stephanie Calmenson. Copyright © 2000 by Stephanie Calmenson. Reprinted by permission of Marian Reiner for the author.

VIVIAN GOULED. "Crossing the Street" by Vivian Gouled. Copyright © 1990 by Scholastic Inc. Used by permission of the publisher.

EVA GRANT. "Wake Up" by Eva Grant. Copyright © 1990 by Scholastic Inc. Used by permission of the publisher.

SANDRA LIATSOS. "My Friend" and "Ice Cream Man" by Sandra Liatsos. Copyright © 2000 by Sandra Liatsos. Used by permission of Marian Reiner for the author.

EVE MERRIAM. "Supermarket, Supermarket" from A WORD OR TWO WITH YOU by Eve Merriam. Copyright © 1981 by Eve Merriam. "It Fell in the City" is the originally untitled poem that starts with that line from BLACKBERRY INK by Eve Merriam (Morrow Jr. Books). Copyright © 1985 by Eve Merriam. Both are reprinted by permission of Marian Reiner for the author.

Notes

SCHOLASTIC

From the Editors at Scholastic Teaching Resources

Dear Reader,

We're always delighted when teachers say, "Your books are the ones we use . . . the ones that go to school with us for a day's work . . . the ones that go home with us to help in planning. . . ."

Your comments tell us that our books work for you—supporting you in your daily planning and long-range goals, helping you bring fresh ideas into your classroom, and keeping you up to date with the latest trends in education. In fact, many Scholastic Teaching Resources are written by teachers, like you, who work in schools every day.

If you have an idea for a book you believe could help other teachers in any grade from K–8, please let us know! Send us a letter that includes your name, address, phone number, and the grade you teach; a table of contents; and a sample chapter or activities (along with color photos, if you have them), to:

Manuscript Editor
Scholastic Teaching Resources
557 Broadway
New York, NY 10012

Please include a self-addressed, stamped envelope large enough to hold your materials.

We look forward to hearing from you!

—The Editors

The Great BIG Book of ★ Thematic Poetry ★

Add pizzazz to thematic units, daily lessons, and shared-reading time with this BIG collection of easy-to-read poems selected especially for young learners! All your favorite themes are here: All About Me, Creepy Crawlies, Farm, Community, Transportation, and Weather. Includes literacy-building ideas for teaching phonemic awareness, phonics and oral language skills, reading, writing, math, science, and more.

Look for these other great books

The Big Book of Classroom Poems
Grades K–3
ISBN: 0-439-43826-8

Pocket Poetry Mini-Books
Grades K–2
ISBN: 0-439-27859-7

Perfect Poems for Teaching Phonics
Grades K–2
ISBN: 0-590-39019-8

Teaching *Resources*

ISBN: 0-439-56729-7
$15.99 U.S./$24.99 CAN.

ISBN 0-439-56729-7
078073567294
X003AIH6CZ

SCHOLASTIC

www.scholastic.com

Top 25 Easy-to-Make Books, Word Walls & Charts for Building Literacy

A Teacher Shares Her Favorite Teaching Tools That Really Make a Difference in Building Skills in Reading, Writing, Spelling, and More

by Heather Getman

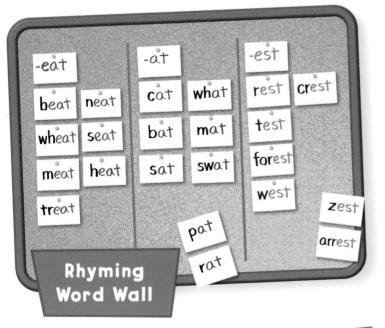

Rhyming Word Wall

Vowels in Our Name Graph

	A	E	I	O	U
25					
24					
23					
22					
21					
20					
19					
18	Jason				
17	Brandon				
16	Christian				
15	Caleb				
14	Michael				
13	Diane				
12	Susan		Christian		
11	Ursula		Christian		
10	Azusa		Judith		
9	Azusa		Michael		
8	Norma		Diane		
7	Zachary	Caleb	Vincent		
6	Zachary	Michael	Liza		
5	Liza	Diane	Jaime		
4	Jaime	Jeremy	Maria	Jason	Judith
3	Maria	Jeremy	Virginia	Brandon	Susan
2	Maria	Vincent	Virginia	Josh	Ursula
1	Virginia	Jaime	Virginia	Norma	Azusa

Graphing Our Names Chart

Build Reading & Writing Skills Across the Curriculum!

A Special Memory For
October
(Month)

We estimated how many seeds were in the pumpkins. There were 553 in the large pumpkin and 458 in the small one.

Name: Jeremy

Special Memories Book

ISBN 0-439-17541-0

51195>

EAN

9 780439 175418

dedications

This book is dedicated to my son, Jackson, whose reliable sleep schedule gave me time to write, and to my husband, Marc, who made me feel like an author.

I'd like to thank all the teachers, children, and parents with whom I have worked, especially those at the Greenacres School in Scarsdale, New York. Special thanks to the children who contributed their work to this book; Ellen Citron, from whom I inherited the activity "Mascot Diary;" and Jim Sullivan and Ed Grossman, who gave me so much confidence as a teacher. My deepest gratitude goes to my principal, Francine Ballan, who encouraged me to write this book and to be the best that I could be, and to my editor, Liza Charlesworth, whose patience and guidance made this book possible.

Special thanks to the children who contributed their work to this book: Abby Augarten, Benny Augarten, Alex Constantin, Rebecca Edelman, Allie Ellman, Allison First, Adrienne Fishman, Sam Kohn, Richard Meyers, Adam Novitch, and Anna Svendsen.

Edited by Louise Orlando
Cover design by Holly Grundon
Interior design by Sally Stilwell
Interior photographs by Heather Getman
Illustrations by Dave Weinberg

ISBN: 0-439-17541-0
Copyright © 2001 Heather Getman

Top 25 Easy-to-Make Books, Word Walls, and Charts

FOR BUILDING LITERACY

**A Teacher Shares Her Favorite Teaching Tools
That Really Make a Difference in Building Skills in
Reading, Writing, Spelling, and More**

SCHOLASTIC
PROFESSIONAL BOOKS

NEW YORK • TORONTO • LONDON • AUCKLAND • SYDNEY
MEXICO CITY • NEW DELHI • HONG KONG • BUENOS AIRES

 Star Word Wall

Purpose:

In order for students to become independent readers and writers, they need to learn the most frequently used words, many of which have irregular spellings. A word wall is a useful way for children to access new words and to become confident in their ability to copy, and eventually internalize, word spelling.

Do This:

1. Create the Star Word Wall by placing the cards for each letter of the alphabet on the bulletin board or wall, leaving space underneath each.

2. Make a list of frequently used words. (See list on page 14.)

3. Write each word on an index card or a sentence strip using a bold black marker. Students should be able to read the words clearly from across the room.

4. Affix a star sticker to each card or strip, if you'd like.

5. File the words alphabetically in a box so that you can access them easily throughout the year.

6. Choose four words each week. Emphasize these words throughout the week during different activities. Have students read the words together, spell them aloud, and make sentences using the words in context.

Skills:
- **Spelling**
- **Alphabetizing**
- **Building sight word recognition**

Materials:
- Card for each letter of the alphabet with a picture that illustrates each sound (A/apple, B/ball, etc.)
- Large bulletin board or wall space
- Index cards or short sentence strips
- Bold black marker
- Thumbtacks or tape
- Shoebox to hold unused words
- Large star stickers (optional)

☺ Why I Like This Activity:

I discovered that this activity conveys to students the importance of conventional spelling. I would not expect them to look up words in a dictionary, but I would expect them to use the word wall, which teaches beginning dictionary skills. As each word on the word wall becomes familiar, students are made accountable for spelling the word correctly in their own stories. When children begin to edit their stories, they are responsible for correcting misspelled star words.

Do This continued:

7. Place each of the four words under the appropriate letter on the word wall, for children's reference throughout the year.

8. Begin the next week by introducing four new words. By the end of the year you will have taught more than 120 new words!

Tips for Success:

✎ Spend the first four weeks of school demonstrating how to use the word wall. Say, for instance, "Listen for the first sound in the word, find that letter on the top of the word wall, and look at the words beneath that letter." This may be difficult at the beginning of the year when some children do not yet have a solid sound/symbol correspondence. Be patient. Model how you would refer to the word wall to spell a word when you are writing on the chalkboard.

✎ To involve parents, tell them which four words you're introducing that week and ask them to review the words at home.

✎ Choose each week's star words in a meaningful way. If you are studying the "silent e" rule, you might choose the words "like," "time," "make," and "came" in the same week to reinforce your phonics lesson. Similarly, you will want to group words with irregular spellings so that they make more sense to students, such as "some/come," "find/kind," or "would/could."

✎ Remember that even at the end of the year, there will be students who have not mastered all the 100+ words that were taught. Mastery of the most common words should be a goal for all students. Exposure to the rest is a helpful head start for the following grade.

FREQUENTLY USED WORDS LIST:

A
and, a, are, as, at, all, an, about, after, around, another, also, any

B
be, by, but, been, back, because

C
can, could, called, came, come

D
do, did, down, day, dear, does, different

E
each, even, every

F
for, from, first, find

G
get, go, good

H
he, his, have, had, how, has, her, him, help, here

I
I, in, is, it, if, into

J
just

K
know

L
like, long, little, look

M
many, more, make, my, made, most, much, man, me, must, may, maybe

O
of, on, or, one, out, other, over, our, only, once

P
people, put, place, part

R
right

S
said, so, see, some, same, such, she

T
to, two, time, too, take, the, that, they, this, there, their, them, then, think, through, than, these, three

U
up, upon, use

V
very

W
write, words, water, was, with, were, we, will, would, way, work, well, what, when, which, where, why, who

Y
your, you

Star Word Books

Skills:
- Spelling
- Listening

Materials:
- Star Word Book cover template (page 17)
- Star Word Book template (page 18)
- Paper cutter
- Stapler

Purpose:

Learning to read and say new words is only part of understanding them. It's also very important for students to learn to write new words. Use this activity in conjunction with the Star Word Wall (see page 13), starting about two months after you introduce your word wall. Give students their own Star Word Book that includes enough pages for one spelling drill each day of the month.

Do This:

1. Determine how many school days are in the month.

2. Photocopy that number of Star Word Book templates to create a packet for that month. Each Star Word Book page and cover template makes two books. Photocopy enough pages for half the number of students in your class.

3. Cut the packet across the middle with the paper cutter so that each packet makes two books.

4. Staple each book with a Star Word Book cover.

5. At the same time each day, ask students to take out their Star Word

These books are an excellent form of assessment. Because the activity is done every day, it does not have the weight of a spelling test, yet it still demonstrates who can use the word wall effectively and who cannot. Children who have consistent difficulty using the word wall will need help developing other strategies for learning the star words.

Do This continued:

Books and write the date at the top of the page. Next, choose a word from the word wall and say it out loud on its own and use it in a sentence. Ask students to write the word either by looking at the word wall or recalling its spelling from memory. Try to have the students write four words each day. Be sure to keep your own Star Word Book to track the words you've used.

6. Ask for a student volunteer to collect the word books. Review and correct misspelled words before returning the books the next day. If a word is misspelled, write the word correctly on a line next to the child's word so he or she can see the difference. Share these books with parents each month.

7. At the beginning of the year, words will be repeated often because there are not many words on the wall. This will change as the year progresses. Revisit difficult words periodically. TIP: Combining new words with previously mastered words helps students build confidence.

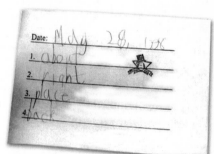

Tips For Success:

✎ Wait to introduce the Star Word Books until the second month of school. By then there will be at least 16 words on the Star Word Wall and students will have had time to learn how to use the word wall effectively.

✎ At the end of each month, make a note of which children had difficulty spelling the star words so that you have a record for report writing.

✎ Encourage students and provide a time for them to review their previous day's Star Word Book page before turning to the next page. This private reflection on their work allows them to internalize any corrections that you made.

✎ Choose words that you notice students often misspell. You may have taught the word "was," yet you continue to see a number of children spelling it "wuz." Assign this word for a few days in a row. Then bring it back for review in a couple of weeks.

✎ Make all the packets for months with the same number of days in advance, clipping them together and labeling them by month. This will save you time making the packets each month.

My
Star Word Book
for

_____

(Month)

Name:

My
Star Word Book
for

_____

(Month)

Name:

Date: _____

★ **1.** _____

★ **2.** _____

★ **3.** _____

★ **4.** _____

- -

Date: _____

★ **1.** _____

★ **2.** _____

★ **3.** _____

★ **4.** _____

Rhyming Word Wall

Purpose:

English-language spelling rules are often complicated, and there are many exceptions to these rules. This exercise covers 32 word endings that are consistent in their spellings, making them the most important for young readers and writers to learn. Teaching students to recognize these word endings will help them spell more complicated words down the road.

Do This:

1. Write each of the following word endings on an index card using a colored marker so that it can be read easily from across the room. (See "Tips for Success" about using the colored markers.)

   at, an, ap, ack, ash, ank
   ot, op, ock
   it, ing, ip, ick, in, ill, ink
   ug, ump, unk
   est, ell
   ate, ame, ake, ale, ay, ain
   ine, ice
   oke, ore
   eat

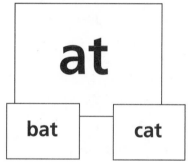

2. File the word endings in the box alphabetically so that you can access them easily throughout the year.

3. Choose one word ending to study each week, posting the appropriate index card on your Rhyming Word Wall. (This is a good exercise to begin on Monday and continue throughout the week.) Ask students to think of words that end with those letters. If the word ending is "at," students might say "cat," "hat," "bat," "Nat," or "that." They might also say "attack" or "attach," which is fine. The word ending doesn't have to be at the end of the word, but it often is with the simplest words.

4. Give students time to think about and write additional words using the particular word ending in their notebooks. At the end of the day (or the next morning), post the words students generated on the Rhyming Word Wall. Keep the words up for the entire week.

Skills:
- Spelling
- Rhyming

Materials:
- 32 5- by 7-inch index cards, with a box to hold them
- Large bulletin board or wall space
- Colored markers (optional)

☺ Why I Like This Activity:

This is a fun, easy activity that helps students understand different spelling patterns. Rather than memorizing a list of words that you give them, the students create their own lists and an interactive bulletin board that includes a range of words, from easy to difficult. I have found that students like the challenge of filling the bulletin board by the end of the week, and everyone gets involved in discussing and spelling new words.

Do This continued:

5. Emphasize the rhyming words throughout the week in your different lessons. By the end of the year you will have taught all 32 word endings.

Tips for Success:

✐ Begin with the easiest word endings and work up to the most difficult (these will vary depending on your students' levels). When possible, coordinate the word ending with the vowel sound you are teaching so that the sound is reinforced. Stick with word endings that share the same vowel sound before moving on to the next vowel sound. You might also choose to teach the word endings with short vowel sounds before those with long vowel sounds.

✐ To help reinforce the sounds, write each word ending with a marker whose color has the same vowel sound. For example use:

- black for short "a" word endings
- pink for short "i" word endings
- purple for short "u" word endings
- orange for short "o" word endings
- red for short "e" word endings
- gray for long "a" word endings
- white for long "i" word endings (either outline the letters leaving a white space in the middle, or use chalk on a black piece of 5- by 7-inch paper)
- gold for long "o" word endings
- green for long "e" word ending

(There are no long "u" word endings.) Some of these color/sound connections are a bit of a stretch, but the colors can really help struggling readers remember the sound.

✐ To involve parents, tell them which word ending you're teaching that week and ask them to review words with their child.

✐ Remember that even at the end of the year, there will be students who have not mastered all 32 word endings. But, students should recognize the connection between the way words sound and the way they are spelled, and many children will articulate, "I know how to spell 'cat,' so I know how to spell 'hat,' because the two words rhyme."

Rhyming Word Books

Purpose:

The Rhyming Word Books are a written record of all the words students discovered for each word ending. Students can review the words at their own pace. Most importantly, the books are a source of pride for beginning readers who find that they can "suddenly" read.

Do This:

1. Photocopy each word-ending template (pages 23-26) at least 50 times.

2. With the paper cutter, cut each page into eighths so you have a stack of slips with a word ending on each slip (these will be called rhyming word slips).

3. Put the rhyming word slips into a box next to your Rhyming Word Wall. Leave an empty box labeled "New Words" next to it. Have pencils available for students, and a table or desk on which they can write.

4. During students' free time, invite them to write as many words as they can think of that rhyme with the word ending of the week. Show them how they only need to write the additional letters (since you've already written the word ending), being sure to put these letters in their correct places. For instance, if the word ending is "ap" and a student would like to write "tap," he must put the letter before the word ending, but if another student would like to write "apple," she must put the letters after the word ending.

5. Once their word is spelled, students should drop their slip into the box labeled "New Words." Each day read the words students wrote the day before. Use the word in a sentence or ask a student volunteer to do so.

Skills:
- Spelling
- Rhyming

Materials:
- Word-ending templates (pages 23-26)
- White photocopy paper
- Paper cutter
- Two small boxes
- Pencils
- Thumbtacks
- Stapler
- Decorated shoe box

☺ Why I Like This Activity:

This activity involves all students. In addition, it encourages cooperation as students support each other to think of and spell new words correctly. The books are very easy to make, yet they represent a great deal of learning. I have found that students begin to take ownership and show pride in the books as they are challenged to think up new words.

Do This continued:

6. If the word is spelled correctly, tack it to the board. If it is not spelled correctly, correct the spelling and explain how and why you did this. Do not put duplicate words on the board.

7. At the end of the week, take down all the words and staple them in the corner with a plain word–ending slip as a cover and write "Words with…." Put these little books in a decorated shoe box that is easily accessible to students.

Tips for Success:

✎ Ask students to write only in pencil so corrections are easy to make.

✎ Encourage students to work on word endings when they finish another activity early. I have my word–endings wall where students line up, so they have something to do while they are waiting.

✎ For crowd control, put out only enough pencils for the number of children that the area can comfortably accommodate.

✎ When you place the words on the board, do it in a meaningful way. Put similar words (such as play, playing, played, and playful) together, and make a separate column for words with blends (like spill, twill, still, trill, and thrill).

✎ Make all the word–ending templates at the beginning of the year and file them so you can pull them out each week to make the slips.

✎ To avoid word duplicates, encourage students to read the words already on the board before writing a new word.

✎ Provide a large stack of word-ending slips at the beginning of each week, but don't feel obligated to replenish it. If students think there is a never-ending supply of slips, they might get silly and write nonsense words. If you have extra slips at the end of the week, save them for next year.

✎ Be prepared for those students who get a kick out of writing inappropriate words. Discourage students from doing this.

at	an
ap	**ack**
ash	**ank**
ot	**op**

ock	**it**
ing	**ip**
ick	**in**
ill	**ink**

ug	ump
unk	est
ell	ate
ame	ake

ale	ay
ain	ine
ice	oke
ore	eat

Alphabet Books

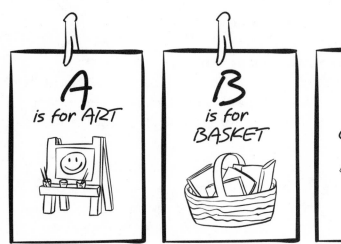

Skills:
• Phonemic awareness

Materials:
• Chart paper
• 11- by 17-inch white paper for each child, plus extras
• Pencils
• Box of permanent black markers
• Newspaper
• Watercolor paints and brushes
• Cups of water
• Clothesline and clothespins or three-hole punch and book rings

Purpose:

Knowing what each letter sounds like is critical to learning how to read. It is not uncommon for students to think that the letter "w" makes the "d" sound because it is called "double u," or that the letter "y" makes the "w" sound because it is called "why." Reading alphabet books and creating your own alphabet book helps reinforce students' awareness of correct letter sounds. This is a great activity to do at the beginning of the year.

Do This:

1. Take out a variety of alphabet books from your school library. Invite students to bring in their favorites from home (be sure to clearly label each book with the student's name). Read a few alphabet books each day. Discuss the different book themes, and invite students to make predictions about a page before you read it.

2. Invite the class to make its own alphabet book. Each child will illustrate one page. On chart paper, list each letter of the alphabet. Discuss a theme for your book. A good theme for the beginning of the year is "All About School."

Once you've selected the theme, ask the class to help you make a list of appropriate objects to illustrate each letter. If there is more than one good idea for each letter, hold a class vote on which object should be illustrated. Ask for volunteers to illustrate each letter.

Here are some recommended titles:

- *Eating the Alphabet* by Lois Ehlert (Harcourt Brace & Co., 1989)

- *The Graphic Alphabet* by David Pelletier (Scholastic, 1996)

- *The ABC Bunny* by Wanda Ga'g (Putnam and Grosset Group, 1933)

- *Flora McDonnell's ABC* by Flora McDonnell (Candlewick Press, 1997)

- *Amazon ABC* by Kathy Darling (Lee and Shepard Books, 1996)

- *The Birthday ABC* by Eric Metaxas (Simon and Schuster, 1995)

Do This continued:

Ask students to have more than one letter in mind because they might not get their first choice.

3. After school, take the sheets of 11- by 17-inch paper and with a pencil lightly draw a line about four inches from the bottom of each sheet. Below the line, write a sentence for that page using a thin black marker. (For instance, "A is for Art Room" and "B is for Blacktop.") Be consistent with the sentence wording.

4. Next, read each page of the book to the class. After you hand out the pages, explain to students that they should first draw their picture using pencil. Later on they will color in their illustrations with watercolors. Encourage students to make their drawings as big as possible. Students shouldn't draw below the pencil line.

5. Before students start painting, you might want to have them draw over their penciled lines with a black marker. (I found that the permanent marker helps control where the paint goes.) Set up a table (or a few desks) with newspaper, watercolor paints and brushes, and cups of water. Have a few children at a time paint their drawings.

6. When the pictures are dry, either hang each page in order on a clothesline for all the class to see or punch holes in the pages and use book rings to make a book. If you plan to make a book, you may want to laminate the pages to make them more durable.

7. Read the class's book aloud. Be sure to include a title page and an author page with all the children's names. If you'd like, students can also add a dedication page.

Tips for Success:

✎ Alphabet books are designed for many different reading levels. It is important to have a wide variety of alphabet books so that readers of all levels can find an appropriate book to read. Encourage children to "read" the pictures aloud if it is a book without printed words. This is an important pre-reading skill.

✎ When choosing a theme for your class book, take suggestions from the class and vote if you'd like, but use your judgment as to whether or not you will be able to think of an object for each letter. Some topics are so specific that it will be difficult to fill every page.

✎ I often make a consonant and/or vowel book instead of an alphabet book and discuss the differences between a consonant and a vowel. This works particularly well if you have 21 children in the class. If you have 22 children, have one child illustrate the cover of the book. If you have more than 26 children in your class, you could make more than one page for each vowel since the vowels have more than one sound. For example, you could make both an "A is for Alligator" page and an "A is for Ape" page.

✎ When discussing ideas for each letter, encourage students to think of it as a collaborative class activity so that no child takes ownership of a particular letter. You want to emphasize that you are making a class book and that every child is an author and an illustrator.

✎ This project can be done over the course of a week, not including the time it takes to read the alphabet books and familiarize children with the format.

☺ Why I Like This Activity:

Alphabet books are predictable and easily accessible to young readers. You can have students make their own individual alphabet books, but the class book serves an important function beyond teaching the sounds of letters. Writing and illustrating a class alphabet book helps create class unity at the beginning of the year, and it also serves to model the collaborative process that will be revisited throughout the year. If you choose to hang the pages of the book, it makes a nice display for open house night.

Stories That Teach Vowels

Skills:
- **Phonemic awareness**
- **Writing**
- **Rhyming**

Materials:
- Chart paper
- Marker
- Photocopy paper
- Thin black markers
- Colored pencils
- Binding machine (optional)

Purpose:

When teaching vowels, it is important to approach the topic in a variety of engaging ways while also reviewing what has already been taught. One way to do this is through creative writing and rhyming. At the conclusion of each vowel study, your class will write a story that relies heavily on that vowel sound. Each student will illustrate a page and finally take a copy of the book home to practice and review sounds. By the end of the year, each student will have five vowel stories that were written and illustrated by the class.

Do This:

1. Review the vowel sound your class has been studying. Explain to students that they are going to write a class story using this sound as much as possible.

2. Begin by coming up with a list of characters for your story. Ask, "Who will be in the story?" (We always use names from our class.) On the chart paper with a marker, write students' ideas under the heading "Characters."

3. Discuss the setting of your story. Ask, "Where will it take place?" "Where should the characters go?" (The stories tend to flow much easier when there is an adventure and the characters are going somewhere.) "What month is it?" "What day is it?" Under the heading "Setting," write the students' ideas.

4. Make a list of words you can use in the story that have the vowel sound you have been studying. Keep reinforcing the sound as you go. Ask, "Do we want any animals in our story?" "Which ones could we have?" "Do we want any food in our story?" "What food could they eat?" "What other words have the sound we are learning?" Write their ideas in columns according to the topic.

5. After a few minutes of brainstorming, your list should begin to show the potential for a story, albeit a silly one. Mold the children's ideas so that their story will make sense. Although you want most of the words in the book to have the vowel sound you are learning, you will need other words, too. Remember, though, that ultimately you want the children to read the

book, so you should keep all the words very simple, using as many one-syllable words as you can.

From your lists of words, you can begin to suggest a plot for the story. You may find that students will continue to make changes and additions as you write the story on chart paper. Try to write one page for each child in the class to illustrate. Be sure each page has something that can be easily illustrated.

6. As you are writing (really transcribing) and revising, keep rereading what you have so far so that all students can keep up with what has been done. Once your story has a clear beginning, middle, and end, your brainstorming session is over.

7. Invite the class to choose a title for the story and a person to whom to dedicate it. Take suggestions for the title and then have the class vote; do the same for the dedication.

8. Hold a piece of white photocopy paper vertically and draw a line lightly in pencil, about four inches from the bottom of the page. You should make one page for each student. Copy the story onto the pages below the penciled line using black permanent marker.

9. Reread the story to your students once, asking them to think about which pages they are interested in illustrating. They should have more than one choice. Then go back and reread each page, assigning each student one page to illustrate with a pencil. Later, they can go over their drawings with a thin black marker. (Remember to include the cover, the dedication page, and the "The End" page.) The illustrations should be outlines so students can color their drawings with colored pencil later.

10. When all the students have finished their illustrations, put the pages in order and photocopy them so that each child will have a black-and-white copy of the book. If you have a binding machine, bind the copies. Do not bind the original. Give students their original drawings back so that they can color them in. When all the pages of the original book are colored, laminate and bind them.

11. Read the class's story aloud and commend your students on their wonderful cooperation and creativity. Put the book on an easily accessible shelf and encourage your students to read it. Give each child a black-and-white copy to take home. Invite them to color their books.

☺ Why I Like This Activity:

This activity helps students learn and practice the writing process (brainstorming, writing, editing, revising, and rereading). It is valuable for students to experience this process in a group setting and to participate with the guidance of an adult. The organized way in which the brainstorming occurs actually teaches children about the elements of story writing. By collaborating, students learn to value each other's ideas and to cooperate with their peers. I have found that students take a lot of pride in the finished product, and by taking the book home, they share that pride with their families. Ultimately, this project allows students to see and hear the sounds they have learned in a meaningful and child-centered context.

Tips for Success:

📎 Brainstorming is inherently a very free and creative experience, but it can become hard to control with a large group of children. Don't be afraid to slow down the process and to use editorial license when necessary. In essence, you are the editor of the book, and you will inevitably have to make some hard decisions about the plot of the story.

📎 Your enthusiasm and excitement are critical in keeping the creative juices flowing. You will discover that students respond immediately to your encouragement and need to hear a lot of, "What a fabulous idea," and "I can't wait to hear what might happen next!" When things get too riled up, you can always say, "Wait, wait, wait! I'm too excited! I can't think about so many great ideas at once!"

📎 Remember that you will do this activity five times throughout the course of the year and there will be significant growth in the children over this time period. The first two times you do the activity, you will be teaching them the process. By the third time, they should be much more independent, not to mention more knowledgeable about the sounds.

📎 I recommend using students' names in the appropriate books to give them ownership and make them feel special. Also, students remember the sounds much better when they associate the sound with a friend's name. To be fair, use a child's name in only one story.

📎 During brainstorming, don't worry if your handwriting gets messy. I am a big proponent of modeling good handwriting, but if you slow yourself down to write neatly, you will certainly miss some of their wonderful ideas. If you ask students to "hold that thought" as you are writing, they will lose enthusiasm and, most likely, the idea as well. Explain that this is a very rough draft and that you will rewrite their ideas more neatly when you make it into a book. It is actually healthy, I feel, for children to see your sloppy writing occasionally, so they appreciate the effort you make when your writing is neat.

📎 Illustrating with marker can be a risky proposition, but explain to students that pencil will not photocopy well. Encourage them to work slowly and carefully and explain that if they make a mistake, they will need to make it into a design because you will not be using white-out on this project. Once you begin to use white-out with children, they'll want to use it on everything!

Mr. and Mrs. Getman on their Trip to Philadelphia

Here is the text from my class's short "o" vowel book. It was our third vowel book, following the short "a" vowel book, *The Pals and the Yak in Africa,* and the short "i" vowel book, *The Pals on Their Trip to India.*

The Pals, the Dog, and the Popcorn
This book is dedicated to Dr. Murphy

Roxie, Joshua, and Molly were friends.

One day in October they went to Roxie's house.

They made popcorn in a pot.

The pot got too hot.

The top popped off.

Then Roxie dropped the pot and…

The kitchen got sloppy!

They went to Yonkers to shop for a mop.

They stopped to take rocks out of their socks.

Then they saw a dog and they named him Oliver.

He had spots and dots.

He was lost and hungry.

They took Oliver home to eat the popcorn.

Oliver ate all the popcorn and got sick!

They took Oliver to the doctor in the hospital.

Oliver got a shot and took a nap on a cot.

Oliver's mom got him and took him back home.

Roxie, Joshua, and Molly looked at the clock.

As they ran home, they saw a dock and a flock of seagulls.

At home, they knocked on the door

and Roxie's mom let them in.

Then she locked it.

Then they played with their blocks.

The End

Then they saw a dog and they named him Oliver. He had spots and dots.

The pot got too hot.
The top popped off.

Hurray for Homonyms!

Skills:
• **Understanding homonyms**

Materials:
• Chart paper
• Thick black marker
• Photocopy paper
• Markers or crayons
• Binding machine (optional)

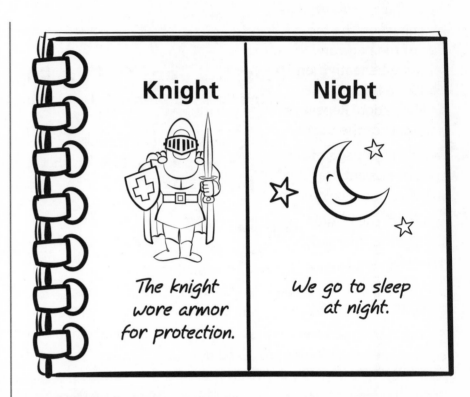

Knight

The knight wore armor for protection.

Night

We go to sleep at night.

Purpose:

Students are fascinated by word play and love to find humor in words that have multiple meanings. As they learn to spell more words, they begin to notice words that sound the same but are spelled differently. This book of homonyms can familiarize students with these unusual words and make learning homonyms more fun.

Do This:

1. Write the word "homonym" on the top of the chart paper using a thick marker. Explain that a homonym is a word that sounds like another word but is spelled differently. Give an example and a sentence to go with each word, such as "We go to sleep at *night*" and "The *knight* wore armor for protection."

2. Ask students to think of other homonyms. Add their ideas to the chart paper. Continue asking for examples, supplying your own if necessary, until you have enough homonyms so that each student can illustrate one.

3. Take a piece of paper for each child and fold it in half horizontally. If a homonym has three spellings divide the paper into thirds. Write one homonym on the top left-hand side of the page and write the sentence beneath it on the bottom left-hand side of the page. Leave space in the middle for an illustration. Repeat with the other homonym on the right-hand side of the page.

4. Reread each page of the homonym book and then give a page to each student. Have them illustrate the homonyms on their page using the colored markers or crayons.

5. Laminate the original pages and bind them into a book. Reread the final product to the class and display it in an easily accessible place.

Tip for Success:

✏ Try this activity whenever the topic of homonyms naturally comes up. You will discover it's not at the same time every year. I've found that discussions about homonyms frequently occur when studying word endings.

☺ Why I Like This Activity:

The project is an easy way to capitalize on students' interest in homonyms and expose them to different spellings and meanings of words. Plus, it's a great way to have fun with language as students challenge themselves to think up homonyms on their own.

Author! Author!

Skills:
- **Comparing**
- **Contrasting**
- **Analyzing texts**
- **Improving vocabulary**

Materials:
- Colored butcher paper (on the roll)
- Thick black marker
- Yardstick
- Several books by a single age-appropriate author
- Chart paper
- 5- by 7-inch index cards
- Markers or crayons
- Masking tape

Purpose:

Reading multiple books by the same author teaches children a great deal about the elements of writing, as well as the valuable skills of comparing and contrasting texts. Through the use of author studies, children learn to express their opinions and give examples to support their theories, both of which are important skills.

Do This:

1. Cut a large piece of colored butcher paper at least five feet long. Put the paper on the floor.

2. With a black marker and a yardstick make and label a chart as shown on page 37. Hang the chart in your classroom where students can easily access it.

3. Next choose an author that you think is appropriate for your students. You may want to start with Eric Carle, Ezra Jack Keats, Tomie de Paola, Rosemary Wells, or Marc Brown. Go to the library and select as many books as you can by your chosen author.

4. Display the books so students can see them. Students may recognize some of the books and be surprised by an author's less popular titles. Students often don't realize that authors write many books. Encourage children to read and look at the books during independent reading. This free exploration helps students become committed to the books on their own level while motivating them for the author-study project.

5. Select five or six stories that you think show a trend in the author's choice of subject, plot, character, or theme. Explain to students that you will use the Author Study Chart to take a close look at a handful of books by a particular author.

6. Show students the Author Study Chart and discuss each of the headings. Define each of the headings on chart paper. Review these definitions often over the course of the project.

7. Read one of the books to the class, keeping the index cards and a black marker handy. You will need five index cards for each book. When you have finished reading, ask the class the title of the

book. Write the title on an index card (held horizontally) and underline it. Then ask who the main character was and write his or her name at the bottom of the next card, leaving room for an illustration above. Repeat for each of the chart headings.

8. Ask for volunteers to illustrate each of the index cards. Only four children will be able to do this each day (the title card does not get illustrated).

9. Using masking tape, hang the students' illustrations in the appropriate boxes on the Author Study Chart. After reading the first book, the first row beneath the headings will be filled. By the time you have read all the books, the entire chart will be full.

☺ Why I Like This Activity:

This project is a good way to build students' vocabulary. As the chart's headings are defined and discussed, the terms eventually become part of the students' own language. Understanding the vocabulary (title, main character, setting, conflict, and resolution) helps students structure their thinking when they are asked to summarize a story they have read or heard. If you ask students to identify the title, main character, setting, conflict, and resolution after reading stories aloud, they will begin to think this way on their own when they are reading and writing their own stories.

AUTHOR STUDY CHART

← 9" →

↑ 7" ↓

	Title	Main Character	Setting	Conflict	Resolution
1	Whistle For Willie	Peter	The city	Peter couldn't whistle	He kept trying until he finally learned
2	The Snowy Day	Peter	Outside, in the snow in the city	The older boys didn't want to play with him	Peter had fun playing alone and with a friend
3	Peter's Chair	Peter	In Peter's apartment	Peter didn't like that his baby sister was getting all his old stuff and attention	Peter realized that he was too big to use old stuff so he gave it to Susie
4	A Letter To Amy	Peter	Outside in the city, on a stormy day	Peter was afraid that Amy wouldn't come to his birthday party	Amy came to his birthday party
5					

Tips for Success:

- When choosing the author, make your decision based on your students' literacy, their prior exposure to literature, and the time of year in which you will be doing the author study. I like to begin the year with an author study and often choose books by Eric Carle or Ezra Jack Keats.

- Choose an author who has written a number of books so that you have more books to choose from.

- You might want to choose an author that is also the illustrator, so students can compare both the text and the illustrations.

- As an extension activity, discuss what a copyright is and check the date on the books to calculate how old the books are.

- Since only four children can illustrate an index card each day, read enough books so that each child will be able to do one illustration for the chart. Keep track of who has illustrated.

- A good author study might take a couple weeks. Aim to read one book and to complete that row on the chart in a day or two. Schedule enough time for students to explore other books by the author in addition to the ones you are studying.

Comparing Stories

Purpose:

By creating the Author Study Chart (see page 37), students learn how to summarize a story by referring to the main character, setting, conflict, and resolution. In this activity, students will compare two stories they read during Author! Author! and decide how they are alike or different. This activity requires more independence than the author study and is also a good tool for assessing students' understanding of terminology, their listening comprehension, and their memory.

Do This:

1. Begin this project after you've completed Author! Author! (page 36). Photocopy the three different templates for each student. NOTE: You will have extra templates because each student will use only one or the other.

2. Ask each student to choose two of the stories that were read aloud during Author! Author! and decide if they are similar or different. They can be stories that are not on the chart, but must have been read aloud to the entire class and written by the same author. Explain that two books can be similar for one reason and different for another reason. Students will have to give examples from the books to show why they think the books are similar or different.

3. Give students time to think about the books that they would like to compare. Some children will know immediately what they want to say. Others will need more time to think. Have the books available so students can refer to them during this period.

4. On one piece of chart paper write the heading "Similar," and on another write "Different." As you call on each student, have the student first tell you if he or she thinks the books are similar or different and why. Write the student's reasons on the chart paper. Since this activity takes more than one day, use these charts to keep track of students' ideas.

Skills:
- Listening comprehension
- Memory
- Comparing
- Contrasting

Materials:
- Compare and Contrast Similar template (page 41)
- Compare and Contrast Different template (page 42)
- Compare and Contrast Illustration template (page 43)
- Horizontal-lined writing paper
- Chart paper
- Black permanent marker
- Markers or crayons, and pencils
- Glue stick

☺ Why I Like This Activity:

This activity gives students the opportunity to express their ideas verbally, pictorially, and in writing. The Comparing and Contrasting Literature Bulletin Board gives you a good insight into your students' level of listening comprehension and their ability to synthesize texts. The project expects a lot from students, but I have found that they rise to the challenge beautifully when given support and guidance.

Do This continued:

5. After school, take the "Illustration" pages you photocopied and write each child's name on the back of one page and each of the titles that he or she chose in the boxes at the top of the page. The next day, ask students to draw a picture to show their ideas. Show them a sample "Illustration" page with the titles written in. Give them an example: *The Very Hungry Caterpillar* and *The Grouchy Ladybug* are similar because they both have main characters that are insects. So under the title *The Very Hungry Caterpillar*, the child would draw a caterpillar, and under the title *The Grouchy Ladybug*, the child would draw a ladybug.

6. Review students' ideas, distribute their "Illustration" pages with the titles written in, and ask them what they will draw to show their ideas. Make sure they know where each drawing should go.

7. The next day, give each student a copy of either the "Similar" or "Different" page. Review their ideas from the chart paper. Work with a few students at a time, assisting them as they use inventive spelling to explain their ideas using either the "Similar" or "Different" page.

8. After school, go over the students' pencil writing with a black marker so that their text can be read from the bulletin board. Use a glue stick to affix each child's "Illustration" page to the top of his or her "Similar" or "Different" page. Hang the students' work on a bulletin board or a clothesline.

Tips for Success:

- ✐ Encourage students to refer to the books when illustrating.

- ✐ If a student draws an illustration under the wrong title, simply white out the titles and reverse them, rather than having the child redo the drawing.

- ✐ If you think this activity will be difficult for your class, use a simpler version that invites all the children to compare the same two books that have been read aloud. Chapter books work well because there is enough information for each child to choose a unique theory.

- ✐ You can easily adapt your "Illustration" template to suit the whole class by writing the titles before you photocopy it.

Title:	Title:

Name:_____

I think the two books are similar because...

_____

_____

_____

_____

_____

Title:	Title:

Name:_____

I think the two books are **different** because...

_____

_____

_____

_____

_____

Title:

Title:

Classroom Classics

Skills:
- **Learning how to retell a story**
- **Improving vocabulary**
- **Creative writing**

Materials:
- A story to read aloud
- Chart paper
- Black marker
- Several sheets of 11- by 14-inch white tagboard or oaktag
- Markers or crayons
- Laminating machine
- Three-hole punch
- Book rings

Purpose:

Listening to stories read out loud helps children develop reading comprehension and vocabulary. After you have read a story aloud, have your class collaborate and write their own version of the story, changing certain aspects to make it more relevant to their lives. The class version of the story becomes a vehicle for developing students' reading and writing skills. (I often do this activity in conjunction with a fairy tale unit since there are so many versions of fairy tales.)

Do This:

1. After reading a story aloud, discuss ways in which you could change the story by using different characters or events. For example, if you read *One Monday Morning* by Uri Shulevitz, you could change the characters from the king and the queen and their entourage visiting a little boy, to the principal and the teachers visiting your classroom.

2. Write students' ideas for changing the story on the chart paper with the marker. Then go through the story page by page, asking students which words you will have to change to make your new version. Transcribe the new text on another piece of chart paper.

3. After school, take the pages of tagboard and rewrite the book with the new text.

4. The next day, reread your students' version of the story. Ask for volunteers to illustrate each page. Collect the finished illustrations and laminate the pages.

5. Punch three holes in each page and use book rings to bind the book. Read the finished product to the class. Invite students to read along with you. If students are interested, have them break into small groups and take turns visiting other classrooms to read their book aloud.

Tips for Success:

✎ I recommend using a big-book version of a classic story. Big books are easier for students to see when they are altering the text.

✎ This activity works best when the story is repetitive, so that only a few words need to be changed on each page.

✎ If the story is not long enough for each child to illustrate a page, let students work together on a page.

☺ Why I Like This Activity:

Students see humor in altering a classic. As they benefit from exposure to good literature, they open their minds to new possibilities for their own creative thinking and writing.

How Many? An Estimation Book

Skills:
- **Estimating**
- **Number sense**
- **Place value**
- **Writing numerals**
- **Counting by 1s and 10s**
- **Understanding volume**

Materials:
- Binding machine or a three-hole punch and three book rings
- 37 copies of the How Many? template (page 49)
- Two pieces of colored construction paper for book covers
- Black marker
- One large piece of tagboard or oaktag
- One large clear plastic jar with a lid (this is the Estimation Jar)
- Black dry-erase markers
- 37 different types of the same small items to fill the jar (see list, page 48)
- At least 40 white paper plates
- Gallon-sized plastic bags
- Large storage box with a lid

Purpose:
Estimating is an important skill that children acquire with practice. By offering students a weekly opportunity to estimate and record their estimations, you provide them with a strong and meaningful foundation in number sense and logic. They also gain familiarity with large numbers.

Do This:
1. With the binding machine or three-hole punch and book rings, bind the 37 How Many? template pages, using the two colored pieces as the covers. Write "Our Weekly Estimations" on the cover with the black marker.

2. On the large piece of oaktag, draw lines to create boxes that are about 2- by 3-inches each.

3. Laminate the piece of oaktag. This will become your Estimation Board. Place the Estimation Jar, the dry-erase markers, and the Estimation Board in an accessible place in your classroom. Each Monday fill the jar with a new item.

September 5, 1997

There were 43 marshmallows.

4. Throughout the week, invite students to write their estimation of the number of items in the jar on the Estimation Board. Estimations should be made anonymously so no one is embarrassed and feels like they're in a contest.

5. Each Friday invite students to gather in a semicircle around the Estimation Jar. Ask for volunteers to count out 10 items, putting each group of 10 on its own white plate. Line the white plates (of 10 items) in a row in front of the class. Together count the filled plates by 10s. When there are 10 plates in a row, begin another row of plates so that there are never more than 100 items in a row. Continue to count by 10s as new plates are added to the row. For example, if there were 220 items, you would count: … 80, 90, 100, 200, 210, 220. You want students to see a set of 100 as a whole unit.

6. When there are less than 10 items left, you cannot fill another plate. Line these "leftover" items on the floor next to the last plate of 10 items so that they are easy to count. If there were 227 items in the final count, you would count: 100, 200, 210, 220, 221, 222, 223, 224, 225, 226, 227.

7. Look at the Estimation Board and see which number comes closest to the actual number of items. Remember, it doesn't matter who guessed the number correctly. Discuss some of the other estimations that were close. Talk about the estimations that were much higher or much lower than the actual number and why this might have been. Compare this week's estimation number with that of previous weeks. Is it a higher number? If so, why? Did the objects' shape or size have something to do with it?

8. Take the estimation book and on the top of the page write the date and at the bottom of the page, write the sentence, "There were (number) (items) in the jar." Say what you are writing as you are doing it and explain why you are writing the number the way you are. For example, if the number of items was 56, you would say "5 sets of ten and 6 more." Write the number 56 next to this.

9. Choose a volunteer to illustrate the items inside the jar on the page.

10. Ask for volunteers to help empty the contents of the plates into a plastic bag for storage. Collect the plates. Wipe the Estimation Board clean with a damp paper towel. You're now ready to begin the activity again.

☺ Why I Like This Activity:

Our Friday estimation activity is one of the highlights of the week because it encourages interesting mathematical discussions and revelations from students. Students are exposed to, and gradually adopt, the mathematical vocabulary and language that indicates their understanding of the concepts. After a few weeks, students begin to really understand estimation, and their estimations become more accurate.

In addition to the mathematical reasoning skills students develop, they learn how to count by 10s. They learn place value and how to write large numbers correctly (fifty-six as 56 instead of 506) as they see the sets of tens and ones. They learn how to describe items based on an item's shape. They are also introduced to the concept of volume. They begin to understand that when an object is larger it takes up more space, so that fewer objects can fit in the finite amount of space in the jar.

Tips for Success:

- It is important that the items in the jar be uniform in size and shape so that meaningful estimations can take place.

- Use items that students know.

- Start with larger items and gradually move to smaller ones.

- Start with round items and gradually move towards more difficult shapes.

- It takes a long time to collect the items you will use in the Estimation Jar each week. I recommend that you collect them over the course of the first year and save them in plastic bags for the following year.

- Using food in the Estimation Jar once in awhile is very effective, but you cannot recycle it for the next year. It is much more sanitary if you use wrapped food, as students will be touching it.

- Allow students to estimate only once each day so that they make a meaningful guess.

- If you suspect that a student intentionally estimates inaccurately (usually in the millions), discuss why such an estimation does not make sense.

- You can reuse the white plates each week.

- Allow only a few children to count items at a time. Otherwise, they get confused and potentially silly.

- In order for the estimation activity to be a successful experience, you need to consistently emphasize that you do not expect students to guess the exact number of items. This may happen occasionally, but it is not the goal of the activity. You simply want to encourage students to make reasonable, educated guesses.

- Encourage students to refer to the Estimation Book before they make their guesses. With practice they will make comparisons to previous weeks and make the connection between the relative size and number of items in relation to previous items.

- To make the estimation activity more challenging, put items with different colors in the jar and have students estimate based on color. They might also sort the items by color, and then add the numbers of each color with a calculator to determine the total.

Sample items to place in the Estimation Jar:

Marshmallows
Clothespins
Walnuts in their shells
Hershey's Kisses
Styrofoam peanuts
Golf balls
Cotton balls
Shells
Chestnuts
Pebbles
Empty film canisters
Pasta shells
Straws
Coin rolls
Unifix cubes
Corks
Peanuts in their shells
Pattern blocks
Pink erasers
Pretzels

NOTE: Keep in mind any allergies students may have when deciding what items to put in the jar.

October 24, 1997

There were 53 clothes pins.

Date: _____

There were _____

_____

_____

10 Black Dots Books

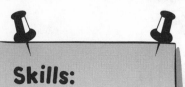

Skills:
- **Retelling**
- **Creative writing**
- **Cooperation**
- **Addition**

Materials:
- 55 circles (2 inches in diameter) made of black construction paper
- 11- by 14-inch paper (one piece for every two students)
- *10 Black Dots* by Donald Crews (Harper-Collins Children's Book Group, 1986)
- Black marker
- Glue sticks
- Crayons and markers

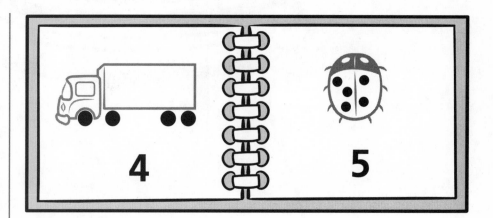

Purpose:

After reading and discussing *10 Black Dots* by Donald Crews, students make their own version of the story. This gives students the opportunity to try their hands at authoring a book. By using *10 Black Dots* as a guide, students focus on specific tasks such as retelling a story rather than worrying about creating a story from scratch. This is a good way to get reluctant readers involved.

Do This:

1. Trace the bottom of a can or other circular object to make 55 black dots. NOTE: If you have more than 20 children in your class, you will need more black dots and you should change the title of your version to "11 Black Dots" (if you have 21 or 22 children), for example.

2. Hold the white paper vertically and draw a line in pencil across each piece, about 4 inches from the bottom.

3. Read *10 Black Dots* and discuss the illustrations. Select children to work together in pairs to illustrate a page of the story. Hand out a piece of the white paper for each pair of children and distribute the black dots. One pair will have one black dot, another pair will have two black dots, another pair will have three black dots, and so on.

4. Have each pair of students discuss and decide what they will illustrate using their dot(s). Once they've decided, ask them to dictate their idea to you so you can write it in black marker below the line you drew earlier.

5. Have each pair glue their black dot(s) to the page and then complete the illustration incorporating their black dot(s). When all the drawings are finished, put them in number order (1 to 10) and read them to the class. The book can be laminated and bound with book rings or hung on a bulletin board or clothesline for display.

Tips for Success:

✐ This is a good activity for the beginning of the year.

✐ You should approve each pair's illustrations before they begin in order to avoid duplication.

✐ Make individual books using round or other shaped stickers of different colors.

☺ Why I Like This Activity:

This activity promotes creativity, cooperation, and compromise, which are important skills in the first grade. The activity also integrates reading, writing, math, and art.

Vowels-in-Our-Names Graph

Skills:
- **Phonemic awareness**
- **Graphing**
- **Counting**
- **Analyzing data**

Materials:
- Colored butcher paper or graph paper on the roll
- Yardstick
- Paper cutter
- 3- by- 5-inch index cards or construction paper in five different colors
- Masking tape
- Black permanent marker
- Red permanent marker

Purpose:

In this activity, students focus on the vowels in their names and graph the total number of each vowel in all the first names in your class. As students complete the activity, they not only strengthen language arts skills, but also math skills as they practice graphing and analyzing data.

Do This:

1. Set up your chart as shown at right.

2. With the paper cutter, cut the colored index cards into 1- by 3-inch strips.

3. Discuss the difference between a consonant and a vowel. NOTE: For this activity we are not counting "Y" as a vowel. Ask students who has a vowel in his or her name. Then ask students if any of them has a particular consonant in their name ("Who has the letter B?").

4. Have students help you find out which vowels are most common in your students' first names. Tell them you will make a graph showing which is most common. Start with the vowel "A." Ask students to raise their hand if they have an "A" in their first name. Invite these students to come to the front of the class and give each one a colored card strip. Have them write their name on the strip and stick it on the graph in the appropriate column with a piece of masking tape. For students with more than one "A" in their

← 6" →

2" ↕

	A	E	I	O	U
30					
29					
28					
27					
26					
25					
24					
23					
22					
21					
20					
19					
18					
17					
16					
15					
14					
13					
12					
11					
10					
9					
8					
7					
6					
5					
4					
3					
2					
1					
	A	E	I	O	U

names, give them additional strips to write their names. For example, Alex would get one green strip, but Andrea would get two green strips because her name has two "A's." Repeat this step using a different color card strip for each vowel.

5. Continue this way until all the vowels have been represented. Pause as you go along to discuss how to read the graph and how the numbers of vowels compare to one another. Ask, "How many more A's are there than O's?" and "Do you think the O's and the U's together are more than the E's? How can we check?"

6. After school, go over the students' writing with a marker. Use red for the vowel that is being counted in each column so that the vowel stands out; use black for all other letters. For example, all the "E's" in the "E" column will be red, while the other vowels in that column are black. In the case of a name that has two of the same vowel in it, on the first strip make the first one red, and on the second strip make the second one red. So the name Elizabeth would have one strip in the "A" column (Eliz*a*beth), two strips in the "E" column (*E*lizabeth and Elizab*e*th), and one strip in the "I" column (El*i*zabeth).

7. Label the graph "Vowels in Our Names," and hang it where everyone can see.

Tips for Success:

✎ Graph paper on a roll is easiest to use because you can just trace the lines rather than measure them.

✎ To make sure the graph will be the right size, count all the vowels in your students' names before beginning the activity.

✎ Children with nicknames need to choose one name they will use throughout the entire lesson so as not to confuse others. Most children choose the longest version of their name so they can be on the graph as many times as possible.

✎ If a child has two of the same vowel in his or her name, place both of that child's strips consecutively, so that students can easily see the first and second occurrence of the letter.

✎ Children may start to get competitive about which vowel is "winning," as if the graph were a race. Emphasize that you are doing an experiment with vowels and that it doesn't matter which vowel is the most common.

Name Graphs

Skills:
- Graphing
- Counting
- Analyzing data

Materials:
- Colored butcher paper or graph paper on the roll
- Yardstick
- 8 1/2- by 14-inch paper
- Paper cutter
- Masking tape
- Black permanent marker

Purpose:

Students create a graph to figure out how many children in the class have the same number of letters in their first names. Students tend to get very involved in this activity, sometimes turning it into a contest. Although I try to stress it isn't a contest, I love that they are getting excited about math topics such as graphing and counting.

Do This:

1. Set up your chart as shown below.

	ONE LETTER	TWO LETTERS	THREE LETTERS	FOUR LETTERS	FIVE LETTERS	SIX LETTERS
10						
9						
8						
7						
6						
5						
4						
3						
2						
1						

‹2"›‹2"›‹ 3" ›‹ 4" ›‹ 5" ›‹ 6" ›‹ 7" →

↑3"↓

2. Hold the 8 1/2- by 14-inch photocopy paper horizontally and use a black permanent marker to draw columns every inch (14 total). Then, use the marker to draw rows every two inches (four total, with 1/2 inch left over). This will be your template. Each template will make four strips.

3. Make enough copies of the template for each child to get one strip, making a few extras. Use the paper cutter to cut the strips so that they are 14 inches long and two inches tall. Throw away the extra 1/2 inch.

4. Ask students to count the letters in their first names and then tell you how many letters they have. Explain to students that you will organize the information they are giving you by creating a graph.

5. Show the class the graph you made earlier and tell the students that you will be keeping track of the information here so that everyone can see it. Show students the strips of paper that have been divided into boxes. Hold the strips horizontally. Explain that each box can only have one letter in it. Demonstrate how to write their names on the strip by writing your name, remembering to put only one letter in each box. Hand out the strips and ask students to write their names on them. Go around the class and cut off the extra boxes that don't have letters in them.

6. Ask students to gather around the graph. Start with the column that says "1 letter." Ask if anyone's name has only one letter in it. If a student's name has only one letter, the student should stick his or her name strip to the appropriate spot on the graph with a piece of masking tape. Continue this way until all names are on the graph. Stop periodically to ask questions about the graph: "How many names have 5 letters?" "Is there any other column that has the same number of names in it?" When the graph is complete, ask students what they notice about the graph. Are there more short names or long names?

7. After school, go over the names with a black permanent marker so that they can be seen clearly from far away. Hang the graph in a prominent spot.

Tips for Success:

✎ If you have a student in your class with a name longer than 14 letters you will need to tape two strips together.

✎ Children may start to get competitive about which number is "winning," as if the graph were a race. Emphasize that you are doing an experiment with the number of letters in their names and that it doesn't matter which number is the most common.

☺ Why I Like This Activity:

This is a fun way to integrate math and language arts. I've discovered that students really pay attention and get excited when the letters we're graphing are part of their names. Without realizing it, students are learning important skills they will take with them to later grades.

Animals! Animals! Animals!

Skills:

- **Research**
- **Reading comprehension using nonfiction texts**
- **Understanding scientific vocabulary**
- **Cooperation**
- **Comparing and contrasting**

Materials:

- Nonfiction books about animals, including dinosaurs
- Boxes to hold the books (one box for each group of four students)
- Construction paper in various colors
- A large piece of colored butcher paper, preferably on the roll
- Yardstick
- Chart paper
- 5- by 8-inch index cards
- Crayons, markers, or colored pencils
- Thick markers

Purpose:

This project gives students a chance to do age-appropriate research using nonfiction texts. Working cooperatively in small groups, students learn about and practice various research skills as they discover interesting facts about animals.

Do This:

1. Divide students into small groups (four or less), taking into consideration the following factors: students' interests, reading abilities (try to mix students with different reading levels), an equal boy/girl ratio, and the likelihood of cooperation among the members of the group.

   For each group, collect at least six books on one type of animal. Put each group's books in a box covered with construction paper (each box should be a different color). Write the name of the appropriate animal on each box

2. Set up your chart as shown on page 58.

3. Begin by creating a list on the chart paper called "How to Read Nonfiction Books." Demonstrate the research techniques included on the list with your own set of research books about dinosaurs. Here is a sample list:

   - Don't read the entire book.
   - It's not necessary to begin reading at the beginning of the book.
   - Use the table of contents (items listed in sequential order).
   - Use the index (ideas listed in alphabetical order).
   - Use the pictures.
   - Read the picture's captions.

4. Discuss the importance of working collaboratively and sharing books with the other members of the group. Demonstrate how two students can share a book. Let students explore the books freely a day before the research formally begins.

5. Each day the class will generate one question to guide the research. All the groups will answer the same question, so it

must be a question that is broad enough to be applicable to all the animals. Write the question on chart paper under a list called "Our Research Questions." You will also write each question on the chart in a box along the top row. I've included some questions on my animal chart sample.

6. After the question of the day is selected, show the class how to find the answer to that question using your box of dinosaur books. Your modeling will teach students not only about dinosaurs, but also about the steps involved in researching a topic. After your demonstration, ask students to move into their groups and begin their own research to answer the same question for their animals. Once they determine the answer to the question, the group should share it with you. Write their answers on the index cards, held horizontally.

7. Have one child in each group illustrate the answer on the index card with crayons or markers, and then place the card on the chart next to the animal's name. After the first day, the first column will be filled with index cards answering the first question about each animal. At the end of each day's research, the groups should share their information with the other groups, so that all students learn about all the animals.

8. After 10 days, the entire chart will be filled and students can easily make observations about how certain animals are similar and different.

Tips for Success:

✎ Due to the amount of reading, independence, and cooperation necessary for this activity, I recommend beginning it in spring.

✎ Choose books with a lot of photographs and captions.

✎ Base your animal choices on the number of available books. Even though students may be very interested in skunks, if there are only two appropriate books about them, the students' research will be too difficult.

✎ Choose at least one representative from mammals, reptiles, amphibians, and birds, for more interesting comparisons.

✎ The list of questions should come from students, but it is important to guide them and to use editorial license if you think a question might be too frustrating to research.

Why I Like This Activity:

This is a good activity to teach students how to work cooperatively. With their new animal knowledge, students take the role of teacher as they share what they learned with the rest of the class. Many students even begin to sound like experts discussing their particular animal. This activity also introduces students to scientific vocabulary, such as predator, prey, offspring, herd, flock, etc. Perhaps most significantly, students learn the difference between nonfiction and fiction.

✎ The groups should always meet in the same spot to do their research to avoid conflict.

✎ Keep track of which children have already had a chance to illustrate the index cards for the chart and do not allow second turns until everyone has had a first turn.

✎ It is helpful to have an adult research book available to check students' research if you are in doubt of a particular answer. Use it sparingly, however; or students may become dependent on you for the answers.

ANIMAL CHART

‹ 9" ›

↑
6"
↓

	WHAT DOES THE ANIMAL EAT?	WHERE DOES THE ANIMAL LIVE?	HOW DOES THE ANIMAL CATCH ITS FOOD?	HOW MANY BABIES DOES THE ANIMAL HAVE?	WHAT OTHER ANIMALS ARE SIMILAR?	WHAT ANIMALS TRY TO ATTACK THIS ANIMAL?	HOW MANY YEARS DOES THE ANIMAL LIVE?	HOW DOES THE ANIMAL DEFEND ITSELF?	HOW MANY OF THE ANIMALS LIVE TOGETHER?
DINOSAUR									
ELEPHANT									
LION									
SNAKE									
GIRAFFE									
SHARK									

Pumpkin Science

Skills:
- **Weighing**
- **Measuring**
- **Predicting**
- **Estimating**
- **Graphing**

Materials:
- Three large pumpkins (one with very defined vertical lines)
- Three small pumpkins (one with very defined vertical lines)
- One medium pumpkin
- Large roll of graph paper
- Newspaper
- Two bowls large enough to hold pumpkin seeds
- Elmer's glue
- Bucket large enough to hold a small pumpkin
- 3- by 5-inch white index cards
- Paper plates
- Chart paper
- Bathroom scale
- Empty half-pint milk carton for each child in the class
- Green construction paper
- Markers for students
- Orange markers or crayons
- Black marker
- Stapler
- Two plastic tubs
- Potting soil
- Bucket of warm, soapy water (if you don't have a sink)
- Paper towels
- Garbage can
- Watering can

Purpose:

This is a wonderful October activity that involves parents coming to school to assist in pumpkin-related science experiments. Preparation for each experiment is done as a whole class, but during Pumpkin Science Day students are divided into groups that rotate through the different parent-monitored stations. Every child has a chance to participate in each station on Pumpkin Science Day. NOTE: The Pumpkin Science Day activities can also be done in the classroom over the course of a week, if necessary, without parent involvement.

Do This:

Set up five stations around the classroom for Pumpkin Science Day (instructions are included under each station heading).

SINK OR FLOAT GRAPH

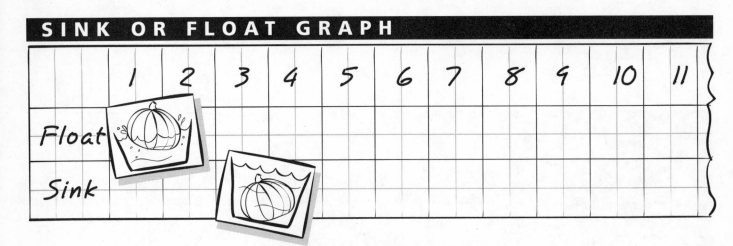

	1	2	3	4	5	6	7	8	9	10	11
Float											
Sink											

Sink or Float Graph:

1. To prepare the graph, cut a long piece of graph paper. Then cut it in half horizontally so you have a long, narrow strip.

2. Set up your graph as shown above.

3. Show students a small pumpkin. Ask them what they think will happen if you put the pumpkin in a bucket of water. Give them a chance to hold the pumpkin. Tell them to keep their guess to themselves so they won't influence their peers. Hand out the index cards. Have students hold them horizontally and draw a picture of the pumpkin sinking or floating, depending on their guess. Place the index cards in their appropriate rows on the graph.

4. When students visit this station, have your parent monitor review the graph of their predictions. Once the entire class has visited the station put the pumpkin in the bucket of water and watch what happens. It floats! NOTE: To avoid a mess, fill the bucket only halfway.

5. Afterwards, compare students' predictions to the actual outcome. Ask students what influenced their prediction. Ask why they think the pumpkin floated. (Pumpkins, melons, and gourds float because they have an air pocket inside. They are not completely solid.)

How Many Seeds Graph:

1. Cut two long pieces of graph paper. These will be used for graphing the predictions of the number of seeds in both a large and small pumpkin.

2. Set up your charts as shown below. Hand out index cards for students to write their predictions.

3. Show students the large pumpkin. Ask them to predict how many seeds are inside. Have them write their predictions on their index cards. Invite students to post their predictions on the appropriate column in the chart. Do the same with the small pumpkin.

4. The day before Pumpkin Science Day cut open the pumpkins and have volunteers scoop out the seeds. Be sure to keep the seeds from each pumpkin separate. Rinse and soak the seeds in water and let them dry on newspaper overnight. Place each pumpkin's seeds in a bowl for Pumpkin Science Day.

5. When student groups visit this station, they should count out 100 seeds from the large pumpkin and put the seeds on a paper plate labeled "100 seeds from large pumpkin." When there are less than 100 seeds left from the large pumpkin, have the group write the number of seeds on their plate (for example, 45 seeds from the large pumpkin). Do the same with the small pumpkin. At the end of the day, count the number of seeds for each pumpkin by the hundreds. Have students compare the number of seeds in the large pumpkin with those in the small pumpkin. Also, compare and discuss students' predictions to the actual numbers.

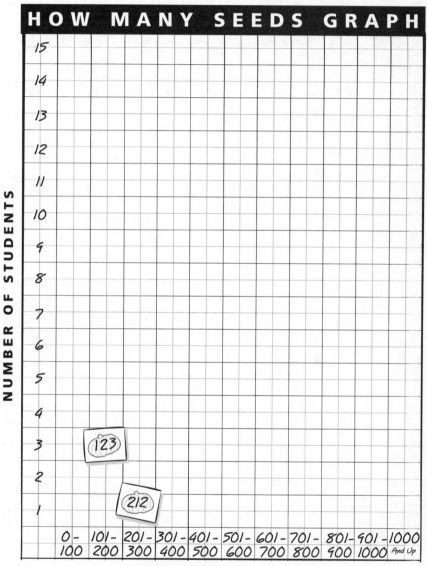

WHICH WEIGHS MORE GRAPH

Which Weighs More Graph:

1. Make the graph as shown above.

2. Before Pumpkin Science Day, place a large pumpkin on the floor. Let students look at it and feel it, but not pick it up. Ask students if they think they weigh more than the pumpkin, the same, or less. Hand out index cards. Have students hold them horizontally and draw a picture of themselves and the pumpkin on a seesaw. Place the index cards in the appropriate row on the graph.

4. When groups visit this station, have them weigh themselves and the pumpkin on the scale. Ask your parent monitor to help students compare the weights.

How Many Lines Chart:

1. To prepare the chart follow the sample to the right.

2. Before Pumpkin Science Day, show students a small pumpkin and a large pumpkin, each with clearly defined vertical lines. Ask students to estimate how many lines they think are on each pumpkin. Have each child come up to the chart and tell you how many lines they think are on each pumpkin. Record their predictions.

3. Ask your adult monitor to help students count the lines on each pumpkin when groups visit this station. NOTE: Create a starting/ending point by making a black dot on one of the lines on each pumpkin.

4. Have the parents lead a discussion about the results. Were they what students expected? Were there more lines on one pumpkin than on another? Does the size of the pumpkin affect the number of lines on it?

HOW MANY LINES CHART

	Small Pumpkin	Large Pumpkin
Steph		
Mike		
Laurie		
Max		
John		
Sally		
Dave		
Erin		
Cadi		
Allison		
Delaney		
Raoul		
Andrew		
Victor		
Tracy		

Planting Pumpkin Seeds:

1. Cut off the tops of the milk cartons. Wash and air-dry them.

2. Measure the height and circumference of a carton, then cut a strip of green construction paper for each child that will fit around the carton.

3. Before Pumpkin Science Day, hand out the strips and ask students to write their names in one section, draw a picture of a pumpkin in another section, write the words "Pumpkin Plant" in another section, and the date in the fourth section. Go over their writing with black marker and laminate the strips. Staple the laminated strips to the milk cartons.

4. To prepare the station for Pumpkin Science Day:

    • Cover a table with newspaper.
    • Fill a box or plastic tub with potting soil.
    • Cut the top off the medium pumpkin.
    • If a sink isn't available, fill a bucket with warm, soapy water.
    • Have plenty of paper towels and a garbage can nearby.
    • Fill a watering can with water.

5. As the groups visit this station, students should find their milk carton and fill it halfway with soil. Next, they should remove six seeds from the pumpkin, place the seeds in their pots, and cover the seeds with a little additional soil. Ask a parent monitor to help students drizzle a little water over the seeds before placing their pots on a windowsill.

6. If a sink isn't available, have students clean up in the bucket of soapy water.

Tips for Success:

✐ Ask parent volunteers to bring the pumpkins and other materials you don't have at school at least a week in advance.

✐ It is time-consuming to make all the graphs each year, so laminate the graphs before you use them the first year so they can be recycled.

✐ Even though it seems excessive, have a different pumpkin for each activity, as specified in the Materials section. Otherwise, the stations will not be able to function simultaneously on Pumpkin Science Day.

✐ Invite parent volunteers to come to the classroom a little early so that you can go over the stations before students arrive. I always have Pumpkin Science Day right after lunch and invite parents during the second half of my lunch hour.

☺ Why I Like These Activities:

This is a productive Halloween activity that involves parents. Each activity integrates math and science meaningfully and shows students how exciting science can be, while helping them feel comfortable taking risks. As students make predictions and form hypotheses, they also strengthen their understanding of numbers.

Thank You Very Much!

Skills:
- **Improving expressive language**

Materials:
- Thankful Book template (page 68)
- Black marker
- Sheet of plain paper
- Binding machine
- Colored pencils for students

Purpose:

Thanksgiving is the first major holiday of the school year. This project serves to crystallize the themes of the holiday by asking students to select something for which they are thankful and then creating a book of their ideas. Copies of the book can be sent home. Parents have told me that the books serve as a springboard for discussion during Thanksgiving dinner.

Do This:

1. Photocopy a Thankful Book template for each child plus a few extras in case of mistakes.

2. Have a discussion with students about what it means to feel thankful. Ask, "What (or who) is special to you?" "What (or who) helps make your life better?" "What (or who) makes you feel happy?" Encourage students to really think for themselves. Although many children are thankful for their families, there tends to be a great deal of variety when it comes to their ideas for this book.

3. Give each student a copy of the Thankful Book template. Ask students to draw a picture and write a sentence or two about what they are thankful for. When everyone is finished, collect the papers. After school go over their writing with a black marker.

4. Alphabetize the pages by students' last names and then bind the pages into a book with a cover. Read the finished book to the class before the holiday.

Tips for Success:

- Reading nonfiction children's books about Thanksgiving prior to writing the Thankful Book helps keep students focused on the origins of the holiday. This is critical to the success of the class book.

- When discussing what makes students feel thankful, steer them away from material things. Emphasize that Thanksgiving is not about TV and toys, but about the Pilgrims surviving their first year in America and overcoming obstacles.

- If you think parents would be interested in the students' ideas, you can photocopy the pages of the book before you bind it.

- Remember to begin the activity with enough time to complete the book by the Monday before Thanksgiving. This way you can send the copies home on Tuesday, in case anyone plans to miss school on Wednesday.

- You may want to add a special poem to the Thankful Book covers. Consider *A Child's Song* by Alice F. Green.

☺ Why I Like This Activity:

I think it is very important for students to be able to express themselves and to acknowledge their feelings in writing (eventually these skills will be used in letter writing). This activity also gives students a chance to feel fortunate as they reflect on their situations.

Name:_____

I am **thankful** for

_____

_____

_____

_____

_____

Draw your picture here.

We Appreciate You!

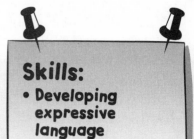

Skills:
- Developing expressive language

Materials:
- We Appreciate You template (page 71)
- Black marker
- Report covers
- Binding machine

Purpose:

Show your students how to say a special thank you to someone who has helped them or made a difference in their lives. Showing appreciation is a learned skill that can be easily taught with this little book. Why not celebrate Nurse's Appreciation Day, Custodian's Appreciation Day, and Aides' Appreciation Day by saying thank you as a class?

Do This:

1. Photocopy one book template for each child in the class.

2. Have a discussion with students about the person for whom they are writing the book. What makes this person special? What does this person do to help students? Why do students like the person? After discussing the person, ask each child to think of a reason why he or she appreciates the person. As each student gives you his or her idea, hand the student his or her copy of the book template.

☺ Why I Like This Activity:

It's very important for students to learn to express themselves and acknowledge the kindness of others. Many students feel quite proud when they share the book with its recipient. This in turn encourages students to show their thanks and appreciation with others. I've also found that this project helps students become more aware of their own actions and understand more clearly how they may affect others.

3. Ask students to draw a picture and write a few lines about why they appreciate the person you are honoring. When everyone is finished, collect the papers.

4. Put the pages in alphabetical order by students' names and bind them into a book with a cover. Present the book to the honoree in front of students. You may want to pass the book around and let students read aloud what they wrote.

Tips for Success:

✐ Students should have some sort of relationship with the person for whom they are writing; otherwise, it will be difficult for them to express any feelings about him or her.

✐ If a child's spelling is not clear, you can write the correct spelling beneath the words in question so the recipient can read it.

✐ You may also want to encourage students to create smaller, more personal books for people they are particularly close to, such as their parents, grandparents, friends, or a babysitter.

Name: _____

We appreciate you because

_____

_____

_____

_____

Mascot Diary

Skills:
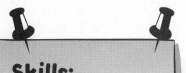

- Retelling
- Reading aloud
- Probability

Materials:

- Stuffed animal
- Canvas tote bag for the stuffed animal
- Composition notebook
- Basket
- Strips of paper with students' names
- Numbered tiles or a deck of playing cards (optional)

Purpose:

Invite a stuffed animal to join your class as a special mascot and watch as students bring the fluffy creature to life. This creative, unusual activity turns diary writing into a fun story-telling activity. Students take turns having the class mascot as a weekend houseguest (in our class it was Tabby, a stuffed dog) and recording his or her adventures in a class diary to be shared with their classmates on Monday morning. Choosing who gets to take the mascot home becomes a lesson in probability as students are picked by lottery.

Do This:

1. About a month into the school year, introduce the stuffed animal. Explain that it belongs to the whole class and lives in the tote bag. During the week, he rests and listens to what is going on in the classroom, but on the weekends, he likes to get out and see new places. He likes to visit with students rather than spend time alone in the school.

2. Show students the class diary (you may want to name it for the mascot, such as "Tabby's Diary") and explain to them that whoever takes the mascot home must write down everything it does during the weekend. The first weekend, you should take the animal home. On Monday, share your entry with the class.

3. On Friday, explain that you're going to hold a lottery to choose a student to take the animal home for that weekend. Reassure students that everyone will have a turn, so it doesn't really matter who goes first. Ask, "Have you ever heard the expression, to pick a number out of a hat?" Fill a basket or bag with numbered tiles or playing cards and show students what the expression means. Explain that the piece you picked was chosen randomly. You will use the same method to choose a student to take the animal home.

4. Write each student's name on a strip of paper. Show the strips to students as you fold each one and drop it into the basket. Pick one strip out of the basket. After a student is picked, throw his or her name away. The chosen student takes the mascot home, records its experiences in the diary during the weekend, and finally reads the entry aloud on Monday to the class.

Tips for Success:

✎ Include a letter to parents in the diary explaining the activity so parents know what you expect. I've found that parents are usually very willing to support the project if they are told how to do so.

✎ "House" the animal in a zippered bag so it doesn't get lost during its travels.

✎ Explain to students (and parents) that the animal should sleep in its bag so as not to spread germs. You may want to wash it a few times during the activity, too.

✎ Do not send the animal home over long weekends or holidays as it is unfair for some children to keep it longer than others.

✎ Calculate the number of two-day weekends in the school year ahead of time so you know when to begin the activity to assure that each child gets a turn.

✎ In my class, students hum the theme to *Jeopardy* to increase the anticipation before a child's name is selected. It serves as a sort of drum roll.

☺ Why I Like This Activity:

This activity is a favorite of my students as they eagerly anticipate their chances of taking home the animal. Students are proud and excited to share their weekends with the class as they practice their storytelling and reading aloud skills. Students who are not immediately chosen quickly realize that as time passes their likelihood of being picked increases.

Special Memories

Skills:
• Retelling
• Reflecting

Materials:
• Special Memories template (page 75)
• Binding machine
• Colored pencils

☺ Why I Like This Activity:

I think these books are a terrific way for students to really think about and remember what was important to them in the first grade. Over the course of the year, the books are also an ideal way to watch students' handwriting and drawing develop. You might even want to encourage students to save these books for years to come.

Purpose:

Each student creates a Special Memories Book, with one page for each month. Every month each student chooses one memory to highlight. As students think about and discuss which activities from the past month were most special, they strengthen speaking, listening, writing, and reading skills.

Do This:

1. Photocopy 10 Special Memories templates. At the top of each page, write the name of each month in the school year.

2. Make a photocopy of these monthly pages for each child. Bind each packet of 10 pages into a book with a cover.

3. As a class, think of 10 or more special memories and write them on the board or chart paper. Review each idea. Ask students to decide which memory is particularly special to them. This will be the memory they add to their personal Special Memories Books.

4. Have students copy the text describing their fondest memory into their books. Invite students to illustrate the memory using colored pencils or other coloring supplies.

A Special Memory for

_____
(month)

_____
_____
_____
_____
_____
_____

Name: _____

Class Yearbook

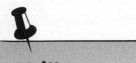

Skills:
- **Retelling**
- **Sequencing**

Materials:
- Camera
- Film
- Large white self-adhesive labels
- Computer or typewriter
- Colored construction paper
- Glue stick

Purpose:

Emphasize the importance of special class trips and experiences by turning a stack of snapshots into a one-of-a-kind photo album. As students create these albums and then review them later, they will strengthen their sequencing, storytelling, reading, and writing skills.

Do This:

1. During your next class trip or special day (such as Pumpkin Science Day; see page 59), snap photos of students in action. Once the film is developed, choose the best photos to include in a Picture This! photo album. Look for photos in which students' faces are visible (not covered by hands or hair), students are involved in the experience, and the location is obvious (you may want to take a picture of a landmark in order to remember the spot).

2. Ask a few students to help you sequence the photos. Have another group of students review the sequence to make sure the photos are in the correct order.

3. Ask students to help write the text for the photo captions. Type or print the captions on the large labels. Next, match the caption labels with the correct photos.

4. Glue the photos and captions to the construction paper. Encourage students to help with the layout and design of the album. (Use a different group of volunteers for each batch of trip/class experience photos.) If you don't want the album to be too thick, use both sides of the construction paper for your layouts.

5. If there's room, you may want to ask for volunteers to add a colorful border or other design to the album pages. Laminate each page and then bind them into a book with a cover.

6. Read the finished photo album to your class or let students take turns reading it aloud. Add the album to your class bookshelf for students to read and look at during their free time.

Tips for Success:

✎ Make sure at least one photo of every student is included in each album.

✎ Aim for natural, rather than posed, photos. It's not necessary for students always to be looking at the camera.

✎ If you're writing the photo captions without the help of students, take care to use vocabulary and sentence structure with which they are familiar.

✎ If you don't have self-adhesive labels, use plain white paper and the glue stick to affix the captions.

☺ Why I Like This Activity:

These photo albums are a great addition to your classroom library. I've found that students (especially reluctant readers) love to read about things that really happened to them. Working closely with students, you can control the content and read-ability of the captions, making them accessible to a wide range of reading levels. Finally, these albums are a good way to share with parents what their children are doing on class trips and special class days.

That's Me!
A Special Year-End Photo Album

Skills:
- Retelling
- Sequencing

Materials:
- Tagboard cut into 9- by 9-inch squares (11 squares per student)
- Camera
- One roll of film (24 exposures) per student
- 4- by 6-inch index card box with dividers
- Glue sticks for students
- Lined paper
- Computer or typewriter
- Large, white self-adhesive labels (20 per student)

Purpose:

Throughout the year, take photographs of students in action, sorting them by child as the rolls are developed. At the end of the year, give students a stack of their own photos to create a special, personal photo album. As students create their albums, they reinforce sequencing skills by placing photos in chronological order and strengthen language arts skills as they write descriptions of each photo. What a wonderful way to reflect on the year!

Do This:

1. Bind 11 pieces of tagboard into a book. Make one book for every student in the class.

2. Over the course of the year take photos of your students in action. After you get each roll developed and printed, sort the photos by student. File each student's photos in the index card box under the student's name. Keep a record of how many photos each child has (to make sure all students have the same number). Each student should end up with 20 or more photos.

3. About two weeks before the end of the school year give each student his or her photos. Have students sequence the photos

as best as they can so that their photo albums will be in chronological order. To help them keep track, have them number the photos. Hand out the blank photo albums and have students number the pages on both sides from 1 to 20 (starting on the second page).

4. Show students how to use the glue sticks to affix their photos to the correct pages of their albums. They can place photos horizontally, vertically, or at angles—encourage them to be creative. Ask students to leave a space on each page for their photo description. Depending on how they placed their photos, the label might go on the top, bottom, or side of each page.

5. Once all the photos are glued into their albums, students are ready to write their photo descriptions. Give students lined paper numbered 1 through 20; allot three or four lines per number, including a line for the title. This will help students stay organized. Encourage students to be as descriptive as possible.

6. As students finish their descriptions, type or print their text, including the photo/text numbers, onto the large labels. Give students the completed labels. Before they stick them in their albums, they should reread each label and make sure it's the appropriate description for the photo. When the albums are complete, have students share them with their classmates.

☺ Why I Like This Activity:

These photo albums are a wonderful way to celebrate the year together and to commemorate students' shared experiences. The project provides year-end closure, which is helpful for a lot of students who have anxiety about moving on to the next grade. Finally, the photo album is a special way for students to communicate with their families about their experiences at school.

Tips for Success:

✎ Ask each student to bring in a roll of film at the beginning of the year. You might want to send a note home, describing the project to parents.

✎ Paying for the developing of the photos can quickly add up. In the past, class parents have volunteered to help with the cost, I've used money that I've received from the PTA, or I've paid for it myself. It never hurts to ask your local photo store for a discount, too.

✎ You can also use Polaroid film. If you do, I would recommend changing the dimensions of the photo album to suit the size of the Polaroid film.

✎ If a photo store offers free doubles, get them, so if you take a picture of two children, you can give each child a copy.

✎ When sorting the photos for students, put their initials on the back of each photo so that when you hand them out they don't get confused about which pictures belong to whom.

✎ Use a larger binding than you normally would for the number of pages in the book, because the photos make the album a lot thicker.

✎ A nice way to decorate the cover of the photo album is with a class picture you take near the end of the year. To save money, take the same photo enough times for half the class to get one. Use the free double offer to get photos for the rest of the class.